Marketing
INTERIOR DESIGN

BY LLOYD PRINCETON

**Allworth
Press**

12 11 10 09   5 4 3 2 1

Published by Allworth Press
An imprint of Allworth Communications, Inc.
10 East 23rd Street, New York, NY 10010

Cover design by Kristina Critchlow
Interior design by Kristina Critchlow
Page composition/typography by Integra Software Services, Pvt., Ltd., Pondicherry, India
Cover photo by Ryan McVayorbis

ISBN-13: 978-1-58115-662-1
ISBN-10: 1-58115-662-6

Library of Congress Cataloging-in-Publication Data:
Princeton, Lloyd.
Marketing interior design / Lloyd Princeton.
   p. cm.
Includes bibliographical references.
ISBN 978-1-58115-662-1
1. Interior decoration–Marketing.   2. Interior decoration–Practice.   I. Title.
NK2116.2.P75 2009
747.068'8—dc22
                          2009011143

Printed in the United States of America

TABLE OF CONTENTS

❖

Acknowledgments

❖

An acknowledgments page is a tough one to write, not because of a lack of gratitude, but because of fear that one or perhaps many deserving people will be left out. So, with an apology to the deserving who have been unmentioned, I would first like to thank Catherine Hiller, my editor and co-author. Without her support, ideas, and good nature, I doubt that I would have embarked on this wonderful journey. So, Catherine, here is a toast to book number two!

Along the way in my career, I have been guided and provided many opportunities to flourish, and there are some key people who have truly been there for me: Charles Grebmeier, John Hale & Hugh Gurley Linda Leach, Sid Goldberg, and my mother, Audrey Princeton— always there at a drop of the hat!

More recently, Sarah Gallop, Bibiana Princeton, David, Winter and John Pujol, each of whom has given me their precious time and support. Naturally, I have to say thank you to everyone who has given me an opportunity to speak, something which is my true passion. And last, my clients, each of whom has trusted me to represent them, provide them ideas, and who have been loyal to the process we embark upon together. While we have not always achieved our goals or ended on a positive note, at least we *tried*. In the words of Albert Einstein, "Nothing happens until something moves." Thank you Justin for sharing this quote with me.

Chapter 1: WHY YOU NEED THIS BOOK

---— ❖ ---—

This book is written for you, an interior designer with your own business. Designers are a creative and talented group, but they often don't know the first thing about the business side of their operations. They may not know how to market their services effectively or have a solid sense of what they are worth. They may even be bashful about setting a price for their work. Raise your hand—or simply blush—if this applies to you!

Furthermore, most designers remain unknown outside their social circle and immediate locale. While your clients may be ecstatic about your work, the rest of the world doesn't recognize your name. This happens because you are an artist, not a business person. You do what you do very well—you create beautiful rooms. What you may not do as well is market yourself. You may not know how to define and publicize your unique style, services, and future professional needs.

The following pages will show you ways to run your business efficiently and discuss strategies to let potential clients, media, and referral sources know about you—a star that is waiting to shine!

In 1999, I started a business, Design Management Company (DMC), because I realized that interior designers are often brilliant at suggesting color palettes but less adept when it comes to avoiding red ink. At DMC, I have counseled dozens of interior design professionals about how they can package their services, create a unique identity that promotes their business, and most importantly, price their creativity appropriately. In these eight years, I have created my own niche as a marketing expert for residential design.

In this book, I will tell you about the business side of your business, including what pitfalls to avoid and pathways to pursue. I will explain to you how to represent yourself to potential clients, how to develop marketing materials (Web site, stationery, brochures, etc.), how to screen and interview clients, how to negotiate the best deal for both of you, how to leverage completed projects for your client and yourself—and much more.

I will tell you what I tell my clients when they come to me for advice.

RAISED LIKE A LADY

One of my first clients, who is still my client today, was an interior designer named Melissa. She lives on the Upper East Side of New York City and caters to a wealthy client base. Her design is distinctive and colorful, and her own lifestyle is similar to that of her clients. In her own words, she was "raised as a lady," so she didn't like to discuss money with her clients. Although she was well positioned to write a letter of agreement before starting her projects, she rarely did so, and when she did, she didn't enforce it. In fact, once I started working with Melissa, she would sometimes discount her services even *after* I had successfully negotiated a terrific deal for her.

Why was Melissa so shy about raising the issue of money? Interior design projects are *all about money*. Rest assured that your clients are thinking about it all the time, so you had better get comfortable with the topic or be able to afford someone who can manage it for you. Remember: how you price your services affects how you will be perceived by your client.

Melissa undervalued her services because she undervalued herself; a common mistake among interior designers and women in general. After reading this book, I hope you will never make that mistake again!

DESIGNING WOMEN

The majority of design professionals are women, and more than 90 percent of my seminar audiences are made up of women. This book is especially addressed to female designers because I believe there are fundamental differences in how men and women do business. I also believe that women can achieve greater success by following the playbook used by men. I think women who read this book will become empowered in their professional dealings and in all areas of their lives.

I am happy to say that today there is a greater acceptance of women as top designers than ever before. The boundaries continue to blur in terms of roles and services that can be performed by either men or women. People are not surprised to work with a male decorator or a female designer. They expect as much from a woman as they do from a man. If the woman designer has established credibility in advance, and if her previous exposure has been highly professional, then she will be treated in a highly professional manner.

It is important to know when you are working as a decorator and when you are working as a designer. If you are freshening up a space with a little bit of color and some new fabric and maybe rearranging the floor plan, then for that project you are working as a decorator. But the minute you order custom merchandise or renovate anything structural (as is usually required for kitchens and bathrooms), you have crossed over to the domain of the designer. Your clients now assume you have the technical skills needed to complete a complex project and should be willing to offer you fair compensation. If design was easy to do and didn't require training, then there wouldn't be the need for special educational and licensing programs, business groups, legislation, and continuing education for practitioners. Design is a multi-billion dollar industry that is very robust. The affluent class continues to buy and refurbish their houses, so the outlook for designers who work with the wealthy continues to be bright.

TODAY'S CHALLENGES

For those working with less affluent clients, residential design is somewhat more challenging for the design professional. Until just a few years ago, residential designers were highly esteemed because they could visualize solutions to problems and discover elusive resources. This has changed with the availability of products and services to the consumer via the Internet. The existence of simple design software, the demystification of the ordering process, and the drop in furniture prices has enabled many consumers to experiment with their own décor ideas without going broke in the process.

What can the savvy designer offer these new, empowered consumers?

Only her talent, experience, and continuing expertise! This is what you must emphasize to potential customers: the years of training and experience that lie behind your suggestions; the knowledge you've acquired on other, similar projects; your innate sense of design. Demonstrate that you are an expert on the materials the project may demand, including green alternatives. Emphasize your knowledge of unusual solutions.

OFFER YOUR VISION

If consumers do not think they need your service or if they do not place much value on your expertise, there is not much you can do to get their business—at *any* price. But if they are persuaded that you are offering a vision and a set of skills that will result in a uniquely beautiful space, they will be willing to agree on a fair price for your work. It is up to you to show them that they need your talent. You must affect their perception of your capability, and you must do so with everything in your marketing arsenal.

I am reminded of a recent media relations account that my firm did not get. This came as a real shock to me, since we regularly land important clients. A group of very savvy designers was planning the national launch of its brand and product line. The designers wanted a firm that could handle the crossover between fashion and interiors (a frequent request at today's top echelons). We interviewed very well and were probably the lead firm at that point. But when it came down to substantiating the talk via our portfolio, we didn't match our competitors. In fact, we were at once the most expensive and the least able to demonstrate what the designers really wanted. The irony is that we actually had the crossover experience, but our press clips did not adequately convey it. Losing the account was an eye-opener for me, and I immediately asked our in-house graphic designer to create an outstanding portfolio that truly represents the value of our services. Experience doesn't do any good if you can't demonstrate it and influence potential clients.

I think that women in particular can learn from this story by making sure that their customers' advance perception is equal to the level of service they wish to provide.

Often, it is the subtle cues that people take that make all the difference. For instance, how available is a designer for an appointment? How flexible is she with cancellations and delays? Is advance payment required? Who is the expert about the subject matter, the designer or client? Who is in control of the interview, the potential client or the designer? To be in charge of a project, you have to take charge of the interview process and establish the value of your time from the get-go. If you let the client lead, then he or she will continue to do so for the remainder of the project, to your detriment. Men have a firmer grasp of this power dynamic than women and continually jockey to stay in the lead, no matter what their role. Women can do the same thing!

Please enjoy the upcoming chapters as we explore ways to enhance your business skills as a design professional.

Chapter 2: YOUR SELF-ASSESSMENT

❖

As you well know (it's probably the reason that you bought this book!), design is not all fun and games. It is a serious, multi-billion dollar global business. It's a growing industry that is currently in flux. Gone are the days of exclusive, trade-only resources. The resources still exist—it's just that your clients probably know about them, too. The industry now has many retail stores with free design services vying for the same clients you want. (We'll return to this topic in chapter 10.) Most likely, there are also other designers in your area. All of this means that you need to be clear about who you are, what you offer, what terms are acceptable to you, and what you want from your career. The questions that follow will help you define yourself and your business. Knowing the answers to these questions will help you make decisions both today and in the future, so grab a pencil and let's begin.

As you ponder your responses, remember: there are no right or wrong answers in this process—or any other creative process. I remember looking at a piece of art with an artist and remarking that one of the lines seemed to go "nowhere" and that perhaps it was a "mistake." He replied, "In art, there are no mistakes." This profoundly influenced me. You need to proceed with the freedom that comes with this knowledge in order to do your best work in all aspects of your life. This certainly holds true as you answer these questions about yourself.

First, every business should have a UPS—no, not a parcel delivery service, but a Unique Positioning Statement. Whether you're manufacturing dolls or treating sewage, there is something special about the way you do it that is part of your UPS. As a designer, your UPS is especially important, and determining it will enable you to present yourself effectively to prospective clients.

Your UPS is central to your pitch—and especially to your "elevator pitch." What would you say about yourself to a stranger in an elevator? This is a very useful exercise when you consider the circumstances involved: a small space, likely with several strangers nearby (maybe *too* nearby), a very short time period (ten to twenty seconds), and the chance to effectively convey what you do. Without practice, delivering an elevator pitch is much harder than it may sound, especially when you factor in the anxiety of public speaking, with everyone in the elevator hearing (and judging) your response.

It's the judgment part that intimidates most of us: "Will they think I'm interesting?" and "Will they be impressed?" Yes and yes again—if you can speak your UPS with conviction, with a smile in your voice, and then ask them something. The conviction conveys confidence, the smile conveys friendliness, and the request conveys curiosity about your target. People always find their own lives interesting, and your showing concern for theirs will make you seem more interesting, too.

It actually took me years to figure out what it is that I do and to edit it down to an elevator pitch. Finally, I came up with the following: "We do marketing and sales distribution for the interior design and home furnishings industry. What do you do?"

Just because it took me years to arrive at my UPS doesn't mean you have to spend that long. Still, it's worth some serious thinking. Developing your UPS is of vital importance because it can be used for:

- **Marketing purposes:** Business cards, Web sites, brochures, and anything that you prepare for your firm.

- **Sound bites:** Interviews with media, in presentations, at parties, and yes, in elevators.

- **Employee training:** One of the most important aspects of an effective UPS, because if your employees are not clear about what you do, how do they know if their efforts are properly directed? How can they answer the phone and direct callers appropriately?

- **Business decisions:** Evaluate business opportunities that frequently present themselves to entrepreneurs by applying them to a strict filter—Is this what we do? Is this our core competency? Remember, just because you *can* do something doesn't mean that you *should* do it.

So, what is your UPS? (Stop chewing that pencil and start marking this book.)

EXAMPLE: *"We do interior lighting for major residential projects, especially homes with extensive art collections that are hard to display. What do you do?"*

66

_____

_____

_____

_____

_____

_____

99

_____

Now that you've developed a first draft of your UPS, ask yourself what your clients can expect when they work with you. Figuring out what clients can expect from you is a good idea: though broad, it will get your creative juices flowing.

EXAMPLE: *They can expect an unusual and sustainable solution to their design problems.*

66

99

Next, consider what you do better than other people in your area. It is worth highlighting any particular skill set, training, or experience you may have. It is certainly important that you have a degree in interior design, because that will always reassure your clients, but for their needs it may be more relevant that you spent several weeks in Italy participating in a mosaic workshop. You might have a specialty that distinguishes your practice from that of other designers. Among the specialties that draw interest today are sustainability, aging-in-place, dealing with allergies to chemicals in the environment, and Feng Shui. Hospitality design is also hot, and giving residences a "boutique hotel feel" is growing in popularity. Be sure to highlight the special knowledge you have about anything, because you never know what note might strike a chord with a potential client. So, what do you do better than anyone in your area?

EXAMPLE: *No one has a better Rolodex than mine for gifted craftspeople. I know the best faux painters, the best upholsterers, and the best stone masons in the state.*

Now, take a look at your present clients. This is an important consideration, since they may represent your interests and core competencies—or not. I recommend scrutinizing the clients you have to see if there is a particular theme or demographic that stands out. You should also ask yourself which clients you have most enjoyed and why. This part of the list is particularly important as you focus your marketing to attract your ideal clients. If you focus on what you enjoy the most, your work will flourish and so will your business. We are not put on this earth for the sake of working; we are here to have purpose, to be of service to others, and to enjoy ourselves in the process. So, who are your present clients and which are your favorites?

EXAMPLE: *A lot of people hire me to design their second homes. I especially like working with clients who are adventurous and are not locked into pre-set ideas of their own.*

66

99

Now ask yourself: What are my favorite projects?

EXAMPLE: *I like working with space constraints and showing my clients how terrific a small house can be.*

66

99

You should take your answers about the clients and projects you enjoy the most to get an idea of your ideal client. What characteristics matter most to you? I know a designer in northern California who enjoys working on multi-year new construction projects with multi-million dollar budgets. She has determined that in order for people to be able to afford this type of project, they will have a net worth of at least fifty million dollars. While this may seem incredible to most designers, it is a realistic target in a country that has the most millionaires of any other country in the world. (According to Merrill Lynch, there are approximately 3,028,000 households in the United States that hold at least $1 million in financial assets, excluding collectibles, consumables, consumer durables, and primary residences.) Moreover, this designer is located in Silicon Valley, which is known for having a disproportionate share of these millionaires—and billionaires, too. You can decide what is ideal for you. This does not mean that you will only take on the clients who fit the mold you are seeking, but when you are uncertain about taking on a potential client, you can apply your filter to help you reach a decision. So, who are your target clients?

EXAMPLE: *My ideal client has just bought a home by the beach, which her family will use in the summer. She doesn't know what she wants; she just knows she wants the house to look and feel a whole lot better. She is eager for my vision.*

As you consider your group of ideal clients, ask yourself about their demographics. Demographics are the statistical data of a population, especially those showing average age, income, and education. To this definition you can also add marital status, estimate of income-producing assets, urbanization (proximity to downtown of a city), and tenure (length in residence and likelihood that they own versus rent). While in your list you may be very clear about what you like, bear in mind that when you seek to find these people through the many data sources available (a topic to which I will return later), the information you will get is statistical: information that is organized and *probably* accurate. So, unless you are given referrals, you are relying on your own marketing efforts. You will constantly strive to refine your approach, your message, and your efficacy. Therefore, get specific as soon as you can to heighten the odds of your ultimate success. What are the demographics you seek for your clients?

EXAMPLE: *I like to create cozy, old-fashioned interiors, so my favorite clients are those that appreciate these. Often these are older people, empty-nesters who now have the money to indulge in their taste for Oriental rugs, marble wash-stands, and carved mahogany furniture.*

It's important to be honest with yourself about why you want to work with a certain group. Listen to your immediate, visceral response: it's a clue as to what makes you tick. Remember, you are self-employed, and you get to decide exactly how you want to run your company, so you might as well run it in a way which is pleasing to you (as long as it's legal). It's best to be realistic about your needs and who you are. Consider the subtleties of personality and the issues of income and lifestyle. Do you work better with people who are detail-oriented and really appreciate your drive for perfection, or do you prefer to work with people who don't fully understand design, but know good design when they see it and let you do what you need to do? Does your ego demand a large budget so that you can spend money the way you really enjoy spending it, or are you content with a small budget that forces you to stretch the boundaries of design and come up with inexpensive and creative solutions?

So ask yourself: why do you want to work with your chosen demographic?

EXAMPLE: *I like working with seniors who want to "age in place." They are always pleased to see how accommodations can work in their homes, and "while they're at it," I often suggest other changes to make the space beautiful.*

16

One of the biggest challenges that residential designers face is the emotional nature of their clients. People can be very involved in their projects (after all, they plan to live there for at least part of the year), and if they work from home or don't work at all, they may torment you 24/7, obsessing over every little detail. This reminds me of the designer who was asked to provide seventeen options for the toilet paper holder in the guest powder room. Worse yet is the client who just doesn't want to make a decision, choosing to wait for a better option, which does not materialize. Here's a tip: if there have been multiple designers on the project before you, chances are your client has a problem with decisions. This doesn't mean you should refuse the job, but you might want to act accordingly. ("I'll need to know which tile you've chosen by Monday so I can show you some washstands.")

It's no wonder that designers rejoice when they get busy, single executives who give them free rein to complete projects and are thrilled with the results. Similarly, more and more residential designers are discovering the joy of commercial work: projects with definite budgets, timelines, and no emotion—you get in, do you work, you get paid. Period.

I firmly believe that there is a match for everyone on this planet, whether it is for love or an interior design project. It's just a matter of taking the time and patience to look for it. If you know that you love to do the detail work that takes a huge amount of time, don't try to do business with people who approach you for a fixed fee because they are worried about being nickel-and-dimed to death. You're not a match. On the other hand, if someone comes to you because they love the detail that they have seen in your work and relish the hunt for the perfect item to complete a masterpiece of a room, then you must quickly tie the knot.

Designers frequently say that they can make do with most budgets and can sell any price sofa. They say they don't need to spend a lot of money to make a room look stunning. But these same designers will turn around and present very expensive items to their clients in the hopes that they will find extra money, beyond the project budget, to pay for the additions. Don't go there! Give your clients what they want and follow your instincts. Be advised that there are plenty of people with money who don't like to spend it and they will try to do the redecorating themselves—though they may call you when they're in trouble. These folks are happy with value-based goods and quality at a reasonable price. Then, there are people who fall into the category of having champagne tastes and beer budgets. Most designers dread this group, but most of us have to work with them anyway, and they give us a chance to display our ingenuity.

What level of service and quality of product are your clients used to receiving?

EXAMPLE: *My clients are a very pampered group and are used to impeccable service. They expect me to be available at all times—my cell must always be on. The upside is they want the best and are willing to pay for it.*

Now, consider your competition. If you do not know your competition, then you cannot properly market yourself. Make a list of the local, regional, national, and international design professionals that you like and emulate and note why you do so. Explore their Web sites and try to understand their philosophies and backgrounds. See what is congruent with your own history, and learn what you share that might help you position yourself more advantageously. Julia Wong, a designer from Calabasas in southern California, worked for the legendary fashion designer John Galliano, traveling the globe for inspiration, before she turned her attention to the world of interiors. If you've ever served as a design assistant who did this sort of scouting, point out your experience on your Web site.

Does thinking about your competition make you feel jealous of the successful designers in your area? A little jealousy might motivate you to do better, but by and large, jealousy is a destructive emotion. You can never be truly certain of other people's circumstances. What you are reading and hearing about is *meant* to sound fantastic—that's what good marketing does. (You, too, can sound great: see chapters 3 and 9.) Remember that the "grass is always greener," and nobody really has it easy. The most successful designers have worked hard to hone their style and their image. So, who is your competition?

EXAMPLE: *To be honest, my competition is the decorator in the store. I have a middle-class clientele, and when they learn of a store's free design service, they often avail themselves of it. I have to market myself to distinguish my style and level of service from theirs. The first step is pointing out that when they use my services, they aren't limited to the furniture that the store provides.*

66

99

What can you learn from the competition? While imitation is the sincerest form of flattery, I don't recommend that you copy everything the competition is doing. However, a little competitive analysis could serve you well. Things to look at include how they structure their firm, the types of projects they work on, where they socialize, which organizations they are involved in, which magazine editors seem to favor them, and so on. It's worth noting how long it has taken them to achieve their success. Chances are it's taken them many years, so don't torture yourself if you're new to the business.

However, there are exceptions to every rule. I am thinking of one of my clients who was born into money. As he tells it, he hadn't realized that he needed to work—ever—until he was well into his twenties and the family textile business went sour. So, he went to school for interior design and worked his extensive social network, developed over the years from private boarding schools and hobnobbing with the elite. In his first year after grad school, he netted—not grossed—$400,000. Sometimes, rather than asking yourself if you can accomplish something, go ahead and ask yourself, "Why not?"—and just go for it.

Now, consider your current situation: you need to have solid footing today in order to build for your future. How did you get to where you are today? Naturally, you know the steps you took to arrive at your current level, but it's good to really explore your past, because you may have something in your background that is not being fully utilized. Many people who come into the field of design are entering a second or third career. They are surprised when I tell them to highlight what they have accomplished before even if it is not design-related. It is important for prospective clients to know that you are not a housewife-turned-decorator (unless you are) and that you accomplished something in business, education, music, raising a family, etc., that adds to your personality and qualifications. Ernie Roth, a designer in Los Angeles, parlayed his career in art direction for television commercials into a successful design practice. While he still works on the occasional commercial to stay in touch with the industry, he spends most of his time designing amazing interiors, using his knowledge of space perception and the technology used for 3-D animation. The best interior designers are often from allied fields, such as fashion, but they may also be from entirely unrelated fields. One very prominent decorator in New York is a former tax attorney with the Internal Revenue Service.

What are your current assets? This list should include tangible and less tangible assets. For instance, if you have money in the bank, or if you own real estate, these are tangible assets. If you are talented, enthusiastic, and are driven to succeed, these are less tangible assets but remain exceedingly important to your overall success. Talent factors into it, too. If you can't design your way out of a box, it will not matter that you own the box. So, list your current assets here:

EXAMPLE: *I'm just starting out. My assets are my degree, my rug-buying trips to Morocco and Turkey, my enthusiasm, and my blog, to which I contribute almost daily.*

66

99

Now, consider where you want to be in your career. How large do you want to get in terms of sales volume and staff? I think this is critical to answer honestly because there is an interesting shift that happens as soon as your company has more than five employees. Often, unless you have an extremely gifted office/business manager in place, you will find yourself doing less design and more management of resources and day-to-day running of your business. This can be frustrating if you enjoy the process of design and are hard pressed to make the time you need to really be a designer, not just a business owner. Of hundreds of designers that I have spoken with, almost all aspire to be the creative directors for their companies and not the CEOs. They want to oversee the creative process while other people execute the design and run the business. It's fun to make things pretty—less so to reconcile a bank statement. With larger companies come increased responsibilities, including office space, human resources, cash management, business development, and paperwork. And if your name is on the door, the buck stops with you, so that means that if you don't find the right people to work with, you might end up being both chief rainmaker and head bottle washer.

So, what are your ultimate goals?

EXAMPLE: *Oddly, I've noticed in my own business that while our revenue continues to climb, so do our expenses. It seems like a never-ending cycle of paying American Express, payroll, and the rent on multiple office locations. But the fact that I don't have to report to an office building—or a boss—makes it all worth it!*

66

_____

_____

_____

_____

99

_____

Now that you've built (or at least designed) your castle in the sky, how will you get from here to there? What are the steps on your stairway to heaven?

EXAMPLE: *I like working with space constraints and showing my clients how terrific a small house can be. I want to be creative director of a design firm that is known for its expertise with small spaces. To do this, I have to reach a special demographic: people with money for a designer who live in small houses or apartments. These might be successful single young professionals or empty-nesters who've just bought smaller homes. I will get to know the realtors who sell them homes. I will get to know my clients in social situations. I will compile an e-mail list of people who could use my services. I will figure out other ways of reaching my target market.*

66

_____

_____

_____

_____

_____

99

_____

The example above focuses on landing new clients. This emphasis is natural; unless we have a patron who is constantly buying and renovating houses, we all need new clients. How do you get new clients at present?

EXAMPLE: *Beats me! Each one feels like a miracle. That's because I've been relying on word of mouth exclusively. I suppose I should be more aggressive about getting new clients.*

66

99

Most designers are not as passive as the one above and have taken some steps to increase their client base. You might have run an ad in a local newspaper or mailed your brochure to people on a certain list. You might have asked your clients to recommend you to their friends. Explore what *hasn't* worked in your efforts to get new clients.

EXAMPLE: *We have a local electronic newspaper with very cheap ad rates. People always say you have to run your ad again and again, so I ran my ad for six months. All I got were inquiries from other designers who wanted to work with me. Later, for just a little more money, I designed a boudoir in a designer's showcase, and I got three new clients in a week.*

66

_____

_____

_____

_____

_____

_____

_____

_____

99

_____

Your design business will only succeed if you are passionate about design. Skills are important, but it is your passion that will attract your clients. In choosing professionals, people often respond for visceral reasons—the gut feeling they get when they meet someone or are given any information to process. I recently read a study that suggests our first response is often our best response, and that our subconscious usually knows our decision ten seconds before we realize it. Think about it. We know what we are going to do before we are even aware of it. I suggest that first impressions are critical and that passion plays a key role in the positive first impression that someone gets from you. How are you communicating your passion?

EXAMPLE: *I send out an electronic newsletter once a month to clients and would-be clients that showcases recent work or experience. In my last newsletter, I included pictures of a living room I had recently completed and wrote about what I had learned about flooring at a recent designers' meeting.*

66

_____

_____

_____

_____

_____

_____

_____

_____

_____

99

_____

In the chapters that follow, I will give you some new ways to answer these questions, and some new ideas about conducting and growing your business. But before we go any further, there's one more question you should answer. If this book does only one thing, it can help you with your answer to this final question. Now, what is the one thing you would like to change about your business right away?

EXAMPLE: *I'd like to arrive at a better and easier pricing formula. I torment myself over losing work because I've asked for too much or losing money because I've asked for too little.*

66

99

Chapter 3: CREATING YOUR QUALITY BRAND

————————————— ❖ —————————————

Everybody thinks they know what a brand is, and most of us acknowledge the importance of "branding." Yet based on conversations with many designers, I wonder if most people understand what a brand really means. According to Webster's, a brand is "a trademark or distinctive name identifying a product or a manufacturer." In interior design services, we are identifying a service provider who has a distinctive style (think Michael Taylor's "California look" or Sister Parish with her chintz). Then there are Jamie Drake with his vibrant colors and Barbara Barry with her refined details. The average designer may not be thinking in these terms. The designer doesn't think he or she will become a household name—but why not?

There is a wonderful expression that says "think globally and act locally." This was coined by the environmental movement, but I am going to borrow it for our needs right now. So, go ahead and think globally: you want to be recognized as a Kelly Wearstler for design so that when people see a cool boutique hotel, they think, "That's Kelly!" So, act locally (get yourself known in your own backyard). For starters, you need to look the part of the person or firm you are try-ing to be. This is not the time for "self-expression": everything about your company has to speak the language of your target market.

WORKING FROM HOME OR GETTING AN OFFICE?

I'm going to start with one the most frequently asked questions my con-sultancy receives: whether to work from home or rent an office. The short answer is it depends. It depends on who your target market is and who your competitors are, because if potential clients are interviewing other design-ers in chic offices, then you had better have one as well. If your clients tend to be stay-at-home moms or dads and don't seem to be interested in your office or never drop by in the first place, then staying at home, the invari-ably cheaper option, will work well for you. I have had the opportunity of visiting both types of set-ups throughout the country and I have been impressed by the organizational efficiency of both. Think of how much more time you can devote to a client if your commute is just up the stairs instead of across town. On the flipside, there are amazing offices that truly impress: expertly designed and well located, with fabulous views. If your clients like this level of elegance, then acquiring it is a necessary step.

You might also want to adopt that real estate mantra, "location, loca-tion, location." One group of design professionals in the Laguna Niguel Design Center in southern California shares a space that is right in the design center. The five of them have their own desks and are exposed to the walk-by traffic of potential clients drifting through the gorgeous center. How smart is that?

WHY GO IT ALONE?

Consider incorporating the resources of other professionals, per-haps ones with whom you can exchange business leads, such as architects, landscape designers, and lighting designers. Also think about owning your space. There is no better way to demonstrate your ability to design than by building out and renovating a space that is yours to do with as you please. Then, you could be in a position to be a landlord to other designers and develop a new income stream. An internationally famous documentary filmmaker I know actually makes most of his income by renting out editing rooms to other film producers. Designers can be in his position as well—or on the other side of the deal. I sublease both of my offices, one from an attorney and the other from a recruiter. Just think of the networking and advice advantages I receive through my rental arrangements. The options are plentiful, and the decision is yours. Just bear in mind what will influence your ideal prospective client.

THE NAME GAME

Next, what will be the name of your business? The easiest and most common option is to name the business after yourself. An eponymous business name identifies you as the proprietor, and if you add the words "interior design" or something related, it tells what you do. My friend Jamie Drake calls his firm "Drake Design Associates." He could take it one step further and add "interior" to the name, but he chooses not to.

When I founded my firm, Design Management Company, I intentionally left my name out of it because I wanted to build an agency that could have many people involved and getting credit for their work. The name says what we do: "design" identifies the industry, "management" is that we provide, and "company," I liked the sound of. However, I missed a critical component in the equation: my speaking engagements. Companies hire me as Lloyd Princeton, motivational speaker, and not necessarily as the firm, Design Management Company. So we modified our name (and logo) to Design Management Company/ Lloyd Princeton for several years. We have since returned to the original name as my career needs have changed.

For design firms, it is important to recognize that whatever name you choose will influence your ability to recruit and retain future talent. David Rockwell is recognized for his company's inventive work in numerous design disciplines. Obviously, he cannot do it all himself; his firm now numbers over 100 people. His business is called The Rockwell Group. By omitting his first name, Rockwell subtly communicates that his associates are important to the "group" enterprise, and that the business is not all about him. This has helped him attract and retain the very best and brightest talent.

LOGO & MATERIALS

Part of your branding or image will depend on your logo and materials. This is a good time to bring in a graphic designer. While many interior designers have terrific taste and vision, those do not always correspond to graphic design, which is truly a specialty unto itself. Much like building a sofa, there are many considerations that go into graphic design. It's much more than the mere placement of information into a space. Consider how long it took you to find the perfect workroom or expeditor. Now tell me how many printers you've worked with. Exactly—probably none. So, find an expert in graphics and let them treat you like a client and provide your business with the full service it deserves. Visit the American Society of Graphic Arts (*www.aiga.org*) to learn more about the field and get names of some local practitioners.

Once you decide on a designer, the first project will be to work with your name. Do you need a logo or do you want a typographic treatment to your name? Do you want a logo that is universally appealing or one that defines (and possibly restricts) your market? I have opted for a typographic treatment to my name, choosing a specific font that we always use in all of our materials.

A logo is nice, but unless you are a major corporation like Nike or Coca-Cola with millions (or billions) to advertise and create an

DESIGN MANAGEMENT COMPANY

LOS ANGELES | NEW YORK | LONDON

DESIGN MANAGEMENT COMPANY | LLOYD PRINCETON

association between your name and the logo, it probably won't matter. So, while you are welcome to create a logo for aesthetic purposes (after all, we are in the business of aesthetics), there is no practical reason for having a logo. But if your graphic designer comes up with a logo that pleases you, go ahead and use it for the psychological lift. The free-lance editor I hired for this book doubts that she really gets more work because of the distinctive long E her graphic designer created for her business, Executive Editor, but Catherine derives pleasure from it as her unique design.

MARKETING MATERIALS

Your marketing materials will include business card, stationery, brochure, Web site, blog, and more. All the graphics should be consistent and create the same overall look. What mood do you wish to convey—conservative, flamboyant, casual, elegant, or whimsical? With six billion people on the planet, there are many different tastes. No one design will appeal to everyone—that is why there are 100,000 designers in the United States alone. So, think about who you are and what type of work you want to be doing, then make sure that the graphics support this mood. Much like the interiors you design, your graphics create an atmosphere and an expectation.

Once you have arrived at your look, the next step is to articulate it across various promotional media, including stationery systems (letterhead, envelopes, business cards, mailing labels, notecards, postcards), brochures, and electronic communications. Remember, before you meet people and introduce yourself to them, their first impression of you may be from one of these items. First impressions can open or close a door very quickly, so put your best materials forward.

BROCHURE? UNSURE!

Some of my designer friends agonize over creating their brochures. I feel that a brochure is usually not necessary. Depending upon the nature of your services and how quickly your firm is evolving, a printed brochure can date very quickly. Any way you look at it, you are going to be spending thousands of dollars to design and print a piece that might only be useful for a short period of time. A Web site will ultimately contain all of this information and more and can be modified at a moment's notice. And while I have seen a few brochures that are truly stunning, the majority are a waste of time and money. If you feel you absolutely must have something in hard copy to hand out besides your business card, consider having your graphics person create one-page tear sheets that are double-sided. You can print them individually on heavy card stock and just run as many as needed. These same sheets are further described in chapter 9 and are used as inserts on projects. In this case, you can add language that describes who you are and the process of your design, and keep them fun. You should also use heavier card stock than you would for multiple sheets in a media kit. Bear in mind that you are designing a piece that will appeal to a prospective client, not you, so let your graphic designer be the objective third party, and consider consulting with a longtime client of yours to see if you are conveying the proper image of your firm.

FOLDER & ENVELOPE

Once you have the stationery system in place, you might proceed with a folder and matching envelope in which to place contracts and presentation materials. The folder exists separately from the envelope, which is used for mailing or to keep the folder clean. Sometimes designers skimp on either the folder or the envelope, but to make the best possible impression, both should be custom printed. I am mentioning this separately from the stationery because folders and envelopes tend to be large items. I paid about $3 for one folder and envelope, and I got a thousand of them

printed, so it can be quite expensive. If you do have the money, creating a matching folder and envelope can be an important way to show that you are serious about business. You can also use them for submission of press materials to editors. If they are memorable, the folder and envelope can help when you make your follow-up calls (see chapter 9).

COFFEE TABLE BOOKS

Sometimes designers are approached by publishers of coffee table books, usually produced by region. Designers are offered an exclusive listing for a specific region, for a cost that averages $1,000 per page and is generally offered in two-page increments (one page might

show rooms you've designed and the page opposite might have your contact info, your bio, and a few words about your inspiration). So, you would be the only Charleston designer in a book that might be called "Southern Interiors." You get a number of books, usually ten, and then have to purchase any more you might use at $50 or more per copy. In this day of inexpensive electronic communications, inclusion in an actual book does confer a certain prestige upon a designer—especially since your clients will not know you have paid for the privilege. If you have exhausted all other marketing avenues or are having a very good year, then go ahead and reward yourself with what I think is something of a vanity project. We are, after all, in a vanity business. Nonetheless, the book becomes less strategically viable when you are reliant upon the publisher to get it distributed, occasionally at book retailers and occasionally at wholesale outlets like Costco. And many copies may go undistributed. It's depressing to wait for the phone to ring from someone who happens to see your design in a book.

Having said this, my firm was not always immune to the lure of such a book. We recently agreed to contribute a client's book. The book was to be part of a gift bag for celebrities on private jets. We were able to gift-wrap fifteen books and put them with a note into gift bags that were waiting on the seats of the celebrities returning from an awards program in Las Vegas. This effort did not result in a single call. In fact, I cannot attest to any designer having received a lead from being in one of

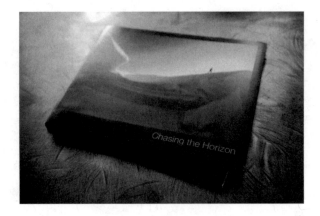

these books. (I would like to hear from you if you have!) If you do proceed, I encourage you to use the copies liberally for promotional purposes, sending them to vendors, real estate agents, architects, editors, and anyone who might be interested in your work or can refer business to you. Nobody ever throws away a photography book. And while you might not get new leads from the book, it will impress prospects who come to your office and happen to see your work between hard covers.

While we are on the subject of photography books, there is another option to consider—publishing your own book. If you have enough quality images to work with, you can use a self-publishing service, many of which produce individual copies very reasonably. This is something that you can update as often as you like and "print on demand." Any well done marketing piece is a step in the right direction, and I have been very impressed with the quality of the self-published books I have seen. I was recently mailed a copy of a self-published book of photographs taken on a trip to Africa. It came to me in a clear plastic wrapping, and it was beautiful.

CREATING A BRAND

Before we leave the topic of brand development, I want to discuss a recent example of a brand that is emerging. Perhaps by the time this book comes out, it will be a success. Two designers who had been designing model homes for many years and were determined to branch out into other endeavors decided to create a brand that is unique to the marketplace in its look and feel—something that is not startlingly original in its style but is entirely unique in its approach. These designers combine interiors and fashion in all that they do, leaving viewers to feel like they have just walked into a fashion shoot. Their presentation books resemble the editorial pages of *Elle Décor* and *Vogue*, and their approach is lifestyle-oriented—they live and entertain the way their clients would expect. I was served lunch in their studio and was very impressed by their attention to detail in the table setting, including monogrammed napkins, iced serving buckets for wine and water, crystal glassware, and silver forks and knives. The whole presentation reinforced the luxurious and fashion-oriented brand that they are marketing. The company is Pal & Smith ... let's see what the marketplace decides.

There are many more examples of designers whose brands are strong and who truly embody what they believe in. Consider Clodagh and her eponymously named firm in New York City. She is the queen of serene and has built a reputation and very substantial business through the use of natural elements in her environments: stone, wood, water, and sustainable materials. When you think of a very cool spa environment, something with calm music and trickling water, think Clodagh. She has developed her brand through her many residential, commercial, and hospitality projects, as well as numerous products in furniture, hardware, lighting, textiles, rugs, and tile that bear her name. Aside from her commercial success, the industry has acknowledged her dedication to her craft and the purity of her designs through numerous awards. Two commercial publishers have produced books about her work: *Total Design: Contemplate, Cleanse, Clarify and Create Your Personal Spaces* (Clarkson Potter), and *Your Home, Your Sanctuary* (Rizzoli). Now that's success!

So what will you be known for? What unique characteristics do you bring to your business, your life, and your clients? Is your current reputation consistent with the vision you have for yourself? If so, terrific—and job well done. If not, then you need to move things in the right direction. It starts with the power of intention: what do you want to happen with your career? Do you want to be wildly successful or do you just want to make a living? While there is no right or wrong answer here, I know that many people reading this book apply self-limits. They doubt the heights they can actually achieve for personal and professional happiness. I figure it is easier to aim higher and accept less than to aim lower and always wonder if you could have been and done more.

AIM FOR THE MOON AND END UP WITH THE STARS

I often look at very successful people in the world, some who are famous because of their public accomplishments and some from the wealth that they have earned, and wonder how they do it. Fortunately, there are numerous books that discuss the strategies, the attitudes, and the ultimate determination that go into success. But for this book, let's just acknowledge that success has to start with the power of intent; more specifically, that you intend to make more of your business than you have thus far, you intend to be recognized by clients, peers, friends and family for what you have accomplished, and you intend to develop a clearly-recognized brand.

Chapter 4: YOUR PORTFOLIO

❖

One way or another, your clients will find you. Maybe they'll find you through referrals or through your marketing efforts. Maybe they'll find you at social or political events. Maybe they'll find you through friends. But finding you isn't enough; you want them to hire you. And generally, potential clients will hire you only after they have viewed your portfolio. In a sense, your projects, whether in actuality or as paper or electronic images, serve as your portfolio and can represent you to the world 24/7.

PHOTOGRAPHY

There is a difference between your actual, "living and breathing" project and your photograph of the project: one can change! Once you sign off on the final walk-through, a client can start living or working in the space you created and change it, often for the worse. Therefore, it is imperative that you schedule your projects to be photographed just before they are completed. In fact, this date should be agreed to in your contract so there is no doubt about the importance that it maintains in your marketing efforts. Sometimes, being able to use the project to promote yourself is as important as collecting your fee.

The best way to demonstrate to new clients what you have done is by showing what you had to work with. Be sure to take "before" shots so you can document the transformation. I think it's fine if you take digital images of each room yourself—you don't need a professional photographer for this. You are just providing a visual record with which to compare your final result, which we presume will constitute a dramatic change. The "after" shots are key to the concept, so proceed cautiously here. It troubles me to see how many designers cannot demonstrate their talent because they have not budgeted for a professional photographer and have used the wrong equipment to capture the wrong angle, with the wrong lighting, of the wrong elements of a room. The images that result are often flat, unexpressive, and, frankly, uncomplimentary. The bottom line is bad photography can make even great design look unimpressive.

The number one reason that designers do not use photographers is expense or the lack of perceived value. Please consider that good photography is inexpensive compared to the money you make from the work your photos help you get. You should hire a photographer who captures the mood of the work that you do. Review his or her portfolio to see that it demonstrates competency in interior (or exterior) photography. The staging, lighting (including time of day, season, etc.), and composition of the image are integral to memorializing your work. We often hear that you have only one chance to make a first impression. These images may turn out to be your chance. In addition, many photographers have relationships with magazine editors and can be instrumental in getting your work considered for publication. You still need to be involved and work with a publicist, but using the right photographer can yield one more plus in the editorial column.

If you target a specific publication, you should check with an editor and see which photographers they work with. Ask for several referrals, since each photographer will have a different price schedule, availability, and working style. You will not know which is right for you until you speak with each candidate. When interviewing, consider negotiating for several projects at once or a long-term contract, say a year. Photographers are like any other business professionals and find it helpful to forecast their cash flow, so often they will offer discounts for multiple projects and commitment.

SCOUTING AND PORTFOLIO SHOTS

There are two types of interior photography: scouting shots and portfolio shots. The difference between the two is the amount of time spent on staging. With scouting shots, images are captured using the basic elements of a room without adding outside influences such as lighting, artwork, and accessories. Ideally, a photographer can do scouting shots in an hour or two and possibly capture several projects in one day. And before you say, "I can do this myself," let me preemptively say, "No, you can't." Get over it! Unless you have worked as a photographer or have won photography contests, just acknowledge the fact that a professional is going to get better images. He or she will make minor lighting and positioning adjustments you might never have considered in order to get the best photograph. You should use scouting shots for projects with which you are not completely thrilled or that do not warrant portfolio shots. It is possible that the scouting images will be satisfactory for your Web site and other marketing uses.

Portfolio shots, on the other hand, are fully staged images that may include outside lighting, products and accessories, floral arrangements, and shots of the designer and clients as well—and don't forget kids and pets! It often takes a full day to capture three or four rooms, let alone an entire project. On top of the photographer's time, you will be responsible for expenses associated with equipment, transportation, and, most likely, a photographer's assistant.

YOUR PORTFOLIO

Once you get the images from the photographer, you will decide which ones best suit the mood of the project and then put them in a portfolio that can be viewed by anyone who is interested. There are many portfolio options from which to choose.

LARGE-FORMAT PHOTOGRAPHY ALBUM WITH HANDLE

This seems to be ubiquitous in the industry, with most of these books being black and about twenty years old. Many of these are the first portfolios ever used by the designers. While they can be convenient to use because the large pages allow instant access to the plastic sleeves, making changes of photos simple, I think there is a lack of permanence with the album. It sends the message, "I just pulled this together and hope you like it," versus the message you want to send: "I am an established business and we take our work seriously." However, if you are stuck on this style, replace the album with a new one when you see signs of wear and tear. Also, only include images of current projects—not your first, just-out-of-design-school achievements.

LARGE-FORMAT BOUND BOOK

If you really want to make a statement, consider a large-format bound book that captures the essence of perhaps one or two projects. One of the best examples I have seen of this type of portfolio is the work of photographer Philip Ennis in New York, memorializing the work of interior designer Robin Baron. The book showed two absolutely stunning projects, with gorgeous imagery, full-bleed, on oversized pages (14" × 13"), bound and imprinted with "Robin Baron Design" on the front cover. The production cost for only the two books was several thousand dollars, not including photography, so it was definitely an investment; however, the impact is unparalleled and truly drives home the message that Robin is a master at her craft.

Small Bound Book

If your budget does not allow you to make this kind of investment (yet), then consider the small bound book. You can get individual books printed from different services, including Kodak and Macintosh, for as little at $35 each with no minimums. They look like small picture books (10" × 8" or thereabout) and are very impressive. They're made with great paper and feature excellent color reproduction. You can print as many as you like and really maximize your marketing power by sending them out to potential clients and media. Now that is impact! It also suggests permanence, quality, and sophistication—all trademarks of a professional designer.

Transparencies

Another option is a series of transparencies: 4" × 5" transparencies that are bordered with 2 inch mat cards. The example I saw was provided by a lighting designer who wants to draw his prospects into the images. Giving prospects transparencies forces them to hold the images up to the light in order to study the details. A stack of them is kept in a box that is presented to the viewer in almost the same way as a gift—as something to open and enjoy. This is particularly germane for lighting, since its effects are often not seen directly, but indirectly, and can make or break a room. A set of transparencies allows you the ease of selecting different projects and only presenting the appropriate ones, an advantage over the bound book.

WEB SITE PORTFOLIO

Let's not forget the most important portfolio: the one on your Web site. Regardless of what you do for your in-person meetings, you absolutely must offer an online version as well. Aside from the fact that you may not get an opportunity to meet in person and present your wares, you benefit from the constant nature of having a portfolio that serves as a business development tool as well. The best part of a Web site is that you have tremendous flexibility with the way you position and size your images, and you can make changes as often as you like. You can add and delete images and text without having to touch the overall design. In fact, it is possible to make many of these changes yourself— once your programmer shows you how. (Much more about your Web site can be found in chapter 12.)

Having said all of this, I would not offer a portfolio until it is asked for. I recommend spending as much time as possible listening to your client's needs, probing for more insights, and then sharing feedback on the process of design as a way to represent your qualifications. Your clients need to know that you hear them, understand what they need, and have the experience and confidence to execute their projects. The portfolio should be an afterthought, really, since what you created for someone else may have nothing to do with what you do for the new client. In fact, your prospects may not see images that reflect what they want, particularly if your portfolio is full of one aesthetic (i.e., traditional), while they are looking for something else (i.e., transitional with a modern interpretation).

EMPHASIZE THE PROCESS OF DESIGN

If you are asked for your portfolio, let your prospects walk through it at their own pace first. Then, when they come to the end, take a moment to highlight things you did that you feel are pertinent to their particular project. If you plan on taking down a wall to enlarge a room, you might point out an image of a situation in which that happened, describing in detail how you went about it through drafts, floor plans, competitive bidding with contractors, etc. During the interview, *keep looking for opportunities to describe the process of design.* (The last is so important I have put it in italics.) This will do two things for you: 1) it will show your competence without giving specific ideas for their project and 2) it will impress upon them how involved design can be and discourage the do-it-yourself projects or the hiring of someone who is not qualified.

I feel that the best portfolio option of all is the project itself. When you don't have images of a project that represents a type of work a prospect needs to see, walk him or her through a previous project. This demonstrates that you maintain good relationships with past clients, gives you more time to get to know the prospect and understand his or her needs, and it shows your talent in 3-D while allowing you to discuss different products—and even pre-sell some of the materials you might want to use on her project. Get the potential client engaged: have him feel the fabrics, sit in the chairs, and touch the surface finishes so the prospect can really imagine what it will be like to live in a room you have created just for him.

Chapter 5: Getting Leads ... and Using Them

❖

"Networking" has become a dirty word. People often tell me, with undisguised pride, that they aren't good at it. For some reason, the idea that you would engage a person in a conversation for other than social reasons carries the stigma of being distasteful.

Now, being social is lovely; being able to meet your financial obligations, priceless. Networking is simply cultivating relationships with people who can be helpful to you professionally, especially in finding employment or moving to a higher position. The reason you bought this book is to move to a higher position, right? So, my goal is to help you understand your cultivation options and let you become more at ease with the concept of networking. Heading a business— any business—requires that you do two things regularly: negotiate and network.

LET'S DO LUNCH

How often have you heard someone say, "I'll call you and we'll have lunch"? How often have you actually gotten that call? Not often, I'll bet! This has nothing to do with intention, as I believe most people are well-meaning and plan to call you at the time, but is rather a function of people being busy, very busy. So, as the person who is trying to develop your network, it is incumbent upon you to reach out to *them*. More than once. Repeatedly. Perhaps many times. For a year or more.

Get the picture? Some of my most lucrative projects are the result of consistent calls, waiting patiently until the timing is right, and then having the service and product needed at the right moment. I have contacted some people twenty times before they have decided to make a purchase. If you head a business, you cannot be shy, and you cannot be lazy. You don't want to be a pest, but you do want to grow your client list. When you are in business, networking and following up with those you meet or hear about is totally accepted—and even expected.

YOUR DATABASE

Being organized, setting reminders, and taking notes are crucial to tracking and following people that you meet. This involves setting up and maintaining a database.

Cultivation of a client database is key for any business. Start with a list of past clients, colleagues, and tradespeople that you enjoy working with. If you have not been in touch with a contact for more than a year, check in by phone to make sure that the contact information is still current. This keeps your list clean: it is counterproductive to send an expensive brochure to the wrong address. Another benefit of this "check in" call is to maintain relationships and remind your contacts about your success and availability. You can tell them about current projects you are working on and the types of jobs that most interest you.

Now, add names you have gathered from your marketing initiatives, including Web site, direct mail, in-store signage (all of which will be discussed later in the book). More names can be purchased from information services companies such as Experian and from mail houses that will sell you a list, print your piece, and mail it for you. All you need to provide is the zip codes and demographics for the people or businesses you want to contact, and they will tell you how many are available under the criteria you select (more about this later).

I use Microsoft Outlook for my database. It integrates my e-mail, calendar, contact records, and a task list. Naturally, it has other bells and whistles that I don't use, but it more than covers the basics. What's nice about it is that I can click and drag e-mails and create contact records, appointments, or tasks, while maintaining the original message in the record. I can also add notes and set reminders so that I know what to say when it is time to follow-up. There are many other such systems available, including ACT, Lotus Notes, and systems integrated with project management software. It doesn't matter which you choose, as long as you have one that can export and import lists for outside marketing efforts, such as sending a list of addresses to a mail house. It's hard to do that from a Rolodex, and your custom-made list in Microsoft Word or Excel is probably not robust enough for the task. If you utilize Outlook or a similar contact management program, you will be able to easily select different formats and fields to upload your files to the various media, including e-blasts, mail labels, and anything else that requires data. You can also easily sort it by categories and the numerous fields you can assign to each contact.

FOLLOW UP

With this in mind, you need to decide on an appropriate course of follow-up once you meet a prospective client. In this era of electronic information overload, a hand-written note or letter can really make you stand out. Of course, you have to have fluid and legible handwriting to carry this off; if you suspect that you don't (few schools have taught penmanship over the last twenty years), you can hand-address the envelope and enclose a print-out—with your hand-written signature, of course. I think an actual hard-copy letter says that you value the person by having taken the time to write them something personal and fold the letter, put it in an envelope, address it, stamp it, and leave your house to mail it. Putting something through the U.S. mail may seem anachronistic with the advent of e-mail and texting, but it's not—it makes a great impression. I remember a recent interview for a media relations account that my firm landed in which the client pulled out a note that I had written a month earlier to one of the decision makers in which I apologized for missing a party. My client told me that the company wanted to do business with a person who took the time to write a sincere letter and actually mail it.

A friend told me how even a trivial letter helped her achieve a major goal. While still a senior in high school, she wrote to a college she was considering, asking about foreign study opportunities. They sent her some materials. She ended up at that college and two years later, applied for their prestigious junior year study-abroad scholarship. When she was told she had won it, the dean pulled out her old letter (they had filed it away before she was even a student) and told her the scholarship committee was impressed by how long she had wanted to study abroad.

AN APPOINTMENT FOR YOURSELF

Another old-fashioned way to follow up is by telephone. (Yup, you can just call them and speak to them by phone!) This gives you the chance to establish rapport, hear the intonation in their voices, and really understand where they are coming from. I always start out my calls by asking, "Am I catching you at a good time?" I never assume that just because people answer the phone they have the time (or the desire) to speak with me at that moment. If it's not a good time, then I ask for the best time to call them back. Frequently, that time is sooner than I would have expected. I make a note that we spoke on that date and then set a reminder to call back on the appointed day. If I'm told to reach someone on a specific day and by a specific time (like in the morning), I will put the call as an actual appointment on my calendar to make sure that I call at the right time. All too often, I have set reminders for myself that roll over to subsequent days and then I miss the window of opportunity to speak with a specific person. Remember, if you want to get something accomplished, set an appointment for yourself—that includes personal things like the gym, shopping for dinner, whatever. You need to block time on your calendar in order to be able to visualize your day and to avoid making commitments that you will not be able to keep, or that will interfere with your accomplishing other necessary tasks.

PERSISTENCE

Over time, you will find that different approaches work with different people. If I have left a few voice messages, I will alternate with an e-mail or an occasional fax, and then, if the person is really not responding, I send a letter through the mail. Sometimes, as I perform these routine marketing tasks, I remember an admonition from my real estate training: "Get off the horse when it's dead!" I have often wondered when the horse *is* dead; when the lead is no longer a lead, but a dead-end. After years of pondering the issue, I have decided that the lead is only a dead-end when the person actually says, "No." Otherwise, the horse is still breathing!

We recently landed a new Web site project with a person who had received over forty telephone communications from us. During that time, there was a false start or two in which the client agreed to move forward and then didn't. One of my associates even left a note in the record to "forget about it." Yet we persisted. That horse wasn't dead: it was just sound asleep.

SHOW UP AND BE PRESENT

Once you are ready to network, you must find the right opportunities for so doing. As Woody Allen said, "90 percent of life is just showing up and being present." Indeed, we are so busy with our lives that it often takes all of the energy we can muster to go to an event—especially in the evening, after work. There are so many events we can busy ourselves with, and it's vital to choose the right ones.

The first step is to determine who your target market is. My target market is design professionals and manufacturers. Next, determine if the event will offer a high concentration of the individuals you seek. Will there be ample opportunity for you to mingle with them? If it's a cocktail party, the answer is maybe; a sit-down dinner, probably so. Who's the sponsor? Is it hosted by an organization or media partner that is reputable? I just went to an event that *Elle Décor* sponsored. I hadn't heard of the showroom, but it didn't matter because the media partner was first-class. Now, consider the cost of the ticket. I have paid from $50 to $1,000 to attend events. The more expensive the ticket, the higher my expectations and the need for the event to produce a return on investment (ROI).

As for charitable events, I am all in favor of donating money and helping worthy causes, but you can't always network and serve a good cause at the same time. Sometimes it happens, but most of the time it does not. If your purpose is to network, then make sure the event offers the right attendees and sufficient access to them. If not, then realize that you are making an altruistic donation, not a business one (even though you can usually deduct the expense for tax purposes), and you still need to get yourself to a networking event. Once again, I'm in favor of charity—but I'm also in favor of generating some cash to support those charitable donations!

Trade Events

People often think that attending trade association events is good for business development. While these events do provide good industry contacts and are often social and educational, they do not really qualify for the heavy networking opportunities that I recommend. You are usually hanging out with your competitors, not your potential clients. These events constitute professional development and can be very worthwhile. It is great to keep learning, as long as you are making money too. However, you need to be aware of your time commitments and how much you have available for social, business, and professional development, as well as community events (including charitable functions). I'm not going to suggest that one is more important than the other, but you need to prioritize these for yourself and determine which to do first and which to attend "schedule permitting."

Personal Interests

Networking opportunities often grow out of your personal interests. People tend to gravitate to and trust people with similar interests and values to theirs. If your interests happen to be in the arts, then attend gallery openings and lectures with receptions. Join councils or groups at your local museums. If you are an outdoors enthusiast, then you can double up by getting your physical fitness in as you network by joining hiking groups, travel clubs, or running clubs and attending equestrian, sailing, or flying events. The last three attract an especially high concentration of people who can afford design services. There are also private social clubs, including country clubs, that lend themselves to golf, tennis, billiards, and the arts. I'm a member of two clubs in New York, the National Arts Club and Soho House; each has a different milieu and purpose, but both have extensive calendars of programs for members. I choose events to attend based on my interest, and then show up. I never know what will come of it. Only last week, I was relaxing poolside at the Soho House when another member who makes custom chandeliers walked in. I casually mentioned that I offer representation to certain designers and manufacturers and had wondered if he would be interested. He called me the very next day! We had first spoken eight months ago and had not done any work together. This time, just in passing, I re-opened the door to business.

Making the transition from social banter to business chatter is less daunting than most people realize. As with any business conversation you are about to have with someone, I recommend asking for permission before beginning. So, in a social setting I will say, "When you're back in the office, there is a) a new service I have that you may find interesting or b) something I need your advice on. When is a good time for me to reach you?" Usually, curiosity will get the better of them (as happened poolside the other day) and they will ask for details right there; occasionally, they will tell you the best day to reach them during business hours. This way you have respected their personal time (and yours, for that matter) and now have permission to contact them, knowing you will get through to them when you call. This takes a minute at most and is exceedingly effective.

Also, assuming they are not juggling an hors d'oeuvre plate and a glass of wine at that moment, you can ask for a business card in order to reach them or write down their number yourself. Here, you are finding out how they prefer to be reached, as some people still avoid e-mail and prefer a call, while others travel so much that e-mails are easier for them. You can offer them your business card as well, which is always good for branding purposes, but always make sure to get their contact information, as well. You should always carry plenty of cards and a pen to write information on the back of the card (such as why you want to contact them). Preferably, you will have eaten before the networking event so that you can focus on who is there, and not on the buffet.

THE SHOWCASE

One way to get leads is by participating in a showcase, if you are asked. Showcases feature the work of a select group of designers who are each asked to customize one room, at their own expense, for a public tour. There are many factors that should influence your decision to design for a showcase. First, consider the reputation of the organization: has it been around for a long time or is it new? If it is Kips Bay (more on that in the next paragraph), then you know it's good; if it's new, then your guess is as good as mine. What you are looking for is consistency and the ability of the organization to deliver on its commitments. Most showcases are run by volunteers, and if they are not well-organized, everyone looks bad. Now consider the sponsoring media—is there editorial coverage you are guaranteed to get? When *Veranda* magazine did a showcase in New York, I knew that the participants would get their rooms published in the magazine. The room you are assigned in a showcase could be good or bad because of its size or location. The living room is great for exposure, but can take a lot of furnishings. The kitchen or the bathroom also provides excellent exposure, but can be expensive due to construction and materials that are left behind. On the flipside, I've seen cute little rooms on the attic levels of houses that typically get ignored—especially when a house is crowded and it's 100 degrees upstairs. The sponsoring vendors and their materials can work for or against you, depending upon the vendor. They get to be preferred vendors by contributing money or product, and in exchange, designers are required to use their wares. This can be good since you typically don't have to pay for the items. It can be bad if you don't like the products.

Finally consider how much cash you will need to fund the project. This is a real wild card. All too often, designers spend 50 percent to 100 percent more than they anticipate on a showcase. First off, you may need to pay an upfront fee of several thousand dollars to participate. Then, you are responsible for all other expenses, including workrooms, product purchases (manufacturers may give you a discount, up to cost, but rarely offer products for free), shipping, installation, etc. All of these add up to your "hard costs." A "soft cost" is your time commitment, for as we know, time=money. Think about how much time it will take for you to design and install your project. In addition, when the house is open, you have to be present in your space for a portion of the time, which may stretch over several weeks. And while you may be able to delegate some of that "babysitting" to staff, you will then need to pay for their time. How much do you charge by the hour? Multiply that by the time you will need to invest and your soft costs could be a figure in the neighborhood of $10,000 or more. So consider all these factors and decide if this investment is prudent for you, with the understanding that the majority of showcase participants never get a new client from the experience.

One of the most prestigious showcases in the country is the Kips Bay Decorator Show House in New York. It benefits the Kips Bay Boys and Girls Club and is the foremost social gathering of the year in the New York design community. Design professionals will jockey for years to get a space and then start out with something very small and hidden, hoping to graduate to a larger room on a more accessible level. The gala opening is an affair to remember, with women in gowns and some men in black tie—lots of glitter and lots of posturing. It's a privilege to participate, and the majority of vendors will donate product to the event. Nonetheless, you will still spend a great deal of time and money to make your space perfect, and then you must hope and pray that people stop and talk to you!

Champagne Marketing

Most major cities have a version of the Kips Bay program. I was in San Francisco recently for the San Francisco Decorator's Showcase, which benefits University High School. I attended the gala opening because one of my clients, Thomas Bartlett, designed the dining room. I was pleased to see that San Francisco gives New York a run for its money. One enterprising designer capitalized on something more visceral than good design—a sexy body! She had an athletic young man wearing a genie outfit (shirtless to show off a smooth, muscled chest) handing out her business cards. By the end of the night, I don't think she had any business cards left, and every time I walked by, she was in conversation with somebody new.

After the opening, Thomas hosted a dinner for thirty of his closest clients, friends, and colleagues—an elegant touch to a grand evening. I can only guess how much this dinner cost him, but I would suggest that additional marketing like this is vital to overall success. You cannot rely on any organization to promote you when they are trying to promote themselves (or raise money) and have many other designers to contend with. You must do most of your own promotion, even if it means pulling out your checkbook.

Collecting Cards

Now, let's assume that you have invested the time and energy to attend an important event. During the event, you must be open to all opportunities, and you must ask for the business card of everyone to whom you speak. (You will, of course, be exchanging your card for theirs, but don't expect that just handing out your card will get you new business.) Carry a pen and make notes right on the card about the context of your meeting and any action required.

By the end of the event, you will have collected a host of names that require some sort of follow-up. First, determine what the appropriate course of action is and who the most appropriate person to contact them is. Perhaps this is not a lead for you, but for one of your vendors or one of your colleagues. Realize that not all leads are meant for you; some may be for people in your circle of influence. I firmly believe in "paying forward."

Pay It Forward

In the year 2000, Catherine Ryan Hyde's novel *Pay It Forward* was published and adapted into a film of the same title. This popularized a concept that was originated by Ben Franklin and further promulgated by Robert A. Heinlein in his book, *Between Planets*. One character offers Don something to eat. Don says, "That's awfully kind of you. I'll pay it back, first chance."

"Instead, pay it forward to some other brother who needs it," the character responds.

The idea is that you spread good deeds around, not necessarily by rewarding the person who helped you, but by doing a good deed for somebody else. If you have a chance to see the movie, you may be inspired to make this your personal philosophy: do something good for another person, and you will be rewarded at some point in time—but not necessarily in like manner or by the same person.

Dealing the Cards

But enough philosophy. Back to that pile of business cards you've extracted from your pocket. If I remember that I had a nice chat with someone and the person is in a position to give me business, then I will give them a call the next day if there is a sense of immediacy to the contact, for example, if they've told me they have someone for me to speak with. If there is nothing pressing for me to follow up on, I might wait a few days to jot them a "nice to meet you" note.

Far too often, I have found myself after a trade show or similar event with several cards that are a mystery to me. I cannot recall why I have them or what faces go with the names. However, I do not let that stop me from contacting them. No matter when the card surfaces, I will send them a note, usually by e-mail in this instance, to initiate contact. My usual e-mail goes something like this: "It was a pleasure meeting you at [event]! In fact, I had so much fun, I completely forgot what I was supposed to do when I got back to my office. I have your business card—is there something I promised to do for you? Hopefully, your memory is better than mine. Please drop a line and stay in touch!" It usually works, and they will tell me exactly what we discussed. Then I add the notes to my database and follow up.

If you attend as many events as I do and find yourself with more than a few business cards on any given day, you may wish to invest in a business card scanner. While they are not perfect, they do scan the information accurately, and then you can adjust the fields, if needed. A scanner prevents you from making transcription mistakes and losing what could be a valuable contact. It's very easy to transpose a digit or add an extra letter to an e-mail address when doing data entry, and once you toss the card, you're out of luck.

The best follow-up with a likely prospect is to meet him or her in person. Nothing beats "face time," or speaking with a person one-on-one. Unless you were sitting next to someone at a dinner party and talking all evening, chances are that you briefly chatted about tangential things. If you determine that you have solid business reasons to know this person better, and if you feel that this is someone who would benefit from hearing your story, then schedule some time for a coffee date. I am partial to keeping meetings simple and not incorporating a meal unless 1) I know that there is a high probability of doing some business with the person or 2) I find them interesting.

MONKEY BUSINESS

Yes, I have also pursued people for another kind of business—monkey business! Romantic inclinations do surface and there is nothing wrong with pursuing them. However, if you want their business, perhaps it is best to just hint that you find them appealing. After all, you usually won't know what they feel, so try to concentrate on business. If you end up working closely together, well, anything can happen then.

Romantic pursuit can go two ways, and unfortunately, you may not be interested in a business prospect who attempts to woo you. The best way to handle this situation is to tactfully keep the conversation directed on business, avoiding any personal details about your life. Usually, the advance will be accompanied by an invitation to get together for a meal, which is dangerous to accept under these circumstances, so you might counter that the best time for you to have a consultation is at the office or during business hours. Or, if the advance is very direct, just say, "I'm flattered and a bit embarrassed. I'm actually involved with someone," or, "I'm not currently dating anybody and prefer to keep it that way." The main thing is: keep it light and help them save face.

LET'S HAVE COFFEE

By keeping a meeting simple and flexible (a beverage is appropriate any time of day, while meals fall into specific time slots), there is less scheduling pressure on both sides. A beverage can be shared in thirty minutes, whereas a meal generally needs at least an hour. Remember that you are sending messages with everything that you do, and you want to be perceived as being busy, all the time. Having a drink rather than a meal also has the benefit of keeping costs down. If you suggest a meal, it does imply that you will pay for it. In wooing clients, I've sometimes spent more money than is prudent because of the restaurant recommendation my prospect makes, and frankly, it hasn't always been worth it. Never be afraid to suggest a place that is more in line with your budget. Even if you feel the other person is obligated to pay because they have suggested the restaurant or invited you, you should offer to split the check. This will end the need for a future meal to return the favor, so to speak.

HELLO AGAIN... AND AGAIN

What do you do with your database once you have a list of names? You need to stay in front of people on a regular basis, at least six to eight times a year. This will keep you on the top of their mind when they are ready to use you. The best way to do this is with a marketing piece that elicits a response from the recipient. One client in New York has an affinity for St. Barts and sent out a letter to his database describing a project that he was working on there, saying that he was looking for other opportunities on the island. Lo and behold, somebody on that list wanted to redo his St. Barts cottage and called him the very next week! You have to ask in order to get.

It's one thing to say hello and reach out and touch them, but it's better to give your potential partners and clients a reason to reach back and touch *you*. That's what direct response marketing is all about—getting the recipient to respond to you. In our daily lives, we encounter this type of marketing constantly, numbing us to all but the very best offers.

THE RIGHT OFFER

The credit card industry has mastered this concept by bombarding our mailboxes with countless types of cards to choose from, changing the offers until we finally get one that appeals to our financial needs. For some people, the lure of lower interest rates is sufficient to trigger an action (balance transfer). For others who don't carry balances, no annual fee or points that are usable in any travel program supply an impetus to apply for the card. Prior to the 2008 credit crisis, a consumer could safely wait for better offers to arrive, knowing that it was just a matter of time until they would receive a variation on the theme that was precisely tailored to their needs. One recent promotion offered two airline tickets to any domestic destination just for charging $500 on the new card. With today's airline fares, who could resist that one? And therein lies the core of direct response marketing: having the right offer that matches the consumer's needs at a particular moment in time.

How do you achieve this symmetry? Through volume. You need to send out vast amounts of material, usually up to a thousand names for each response you want to get. If the offer is truly compelling, you may need to send it out to only a few names to get one response.

40/40/20

In order to maximize your potential with DM (the industry acronym for Direct Marketing or Direct Mail), you need to follow the 40/40/20 rule. 40 percent of your effectiveness will be based on the quality (not quantity) of the database that you use. Do you have the right target audience for your particular offer? The next 40 percent is based on the quality of the offer you are using. Are you offering the target the right offer at the right time? Have you articulated your message in a concise manner so that they know what you are offering, when the offer expires, and what they need to do to respond? And the final 20 percent is based on the quality of the artwork that you use. Are your graphics and layout appealing to the recipient and presented in a manner that engages the eyes, leading them where you want them to go?

Perhaps it's August and you are doing a Christmas promotion. "Order Now for Christmas" (or, more whimsically, "A Partridge in a Pear

Tree") can be the title of a communication that goes out announcing that the custom-made products can take ten to twelve weeks to receive. If someone wants a new dining table by Christmas, they'd better get the order placed in September or risk not having a table in time for their Christmas dinner. You're establishing your authority by pointing out deadlines for obtaining custom furnishings in time for the holiday season, and you're helping your clients avoid the pain of unmet expectations by alerting them to the timeline.

Now let's apply the 40/40/20 rule to this example. The first element is the list. You should include all of your past clients and more—your whole database. Everyone knows somebody who will celebrate the holiday and can use a reminder. The second element is the offer. You'd like them to call your office and work with you to select and order that Christmas necessity. "Call my office by August 15 to guarantee delivery of custom furniture by Christmas." The message is clear and those people with whom it resonates will take the steps required to get their pieces on time. If people fail to place their orders in time, but acknowledge that they knew about the deadline from your communiqué, then you have the option of adjusting your pricing for a "rush" order. Why should their failure to plan ahead create an emergency for you? Charge them accordingly!

The third element is the artwork: perhaps something that incorporates your brand and a holiday symbol, such as a Christmas tree ornament or an angel. If you have a logo, you can "hang the ornament" from your logo or have the angel hover above it. (Consider how Google whimsically modifies its logo for various holidays throughout the year.) And your piece might include a gorgeous image of a festive room that you created in the past and instructions on what needs to happen—by when.

You may have noticed that up until now, I have not said anything about the format of your mail piece (whether it goes out electronically or by U.S. postal service). Both can be effective.

E-MAIL OR "SNAIL MAIL"?

First, let's consider e-mail and its advantages. An e-mail blast can be launched at a moment's notice and is inexpensive to send, averaging pennies an address in overall cost for the campaign. Also, the design can be changed as often as you like. The principal disadvantage is that the mail frequently gets stopped and deleted by increasingly sophisticated spam filters, which look for telling details of bulk e-mail including subject matter, sender, and certain graphics and language. Furthermore, e-mail addresses are harder to obtain from wary consumers, and it's difficult to maintain a clean list because people frequently change their e-mail addresses. I do not recommend purchasing e-mail addressees as they tend not to be accurate nor permission-based—in other words, the person has not agreed to hear from you. Finally, the competition for the reader's attention is staggering. People often do the easiest thing, not the best thing, and the easiest thing to do to a new e-mail is to delete it!

If you decide on an e-mail campaign, be sure to send out your message on the right days of the week (Monday and Friday are less effective) and at the right times (mid afternoon is best, as most people have already cleaned out their inboxes from the evening before). Be sure that your message is laid out with the right balance of text and graphics and that links to your offer work properly, taking the respondent to a landing page so an order can be placed or a request for information acknowledged. The art and science behind effective e-mail campaigns is so specific that a whole industry has sprouted up around it. You might consult with a professional before sending out your first e-mail campaign.

Some say that e-mail, that transformative electronic "time-saver," can actually have an adverse affect on users; e-mail is sometimes seen as the scourge of the business person. So many e-mails are being exchanged and so much spam is clogging our inboxes that people are simply overwhelmed with the volume that they receive. While e-mail is great for many things, it cannot be a sole or major source of your marketing efforts—think spam filters and "no e-mail Fridays."

There are several advantages to sending out your mailing via U.S. Postal Service. First, obtaining accurate addresses from list companies is relatively easy and inexpensive ($80 per 1,000 names). Furthermore, there are no spam filters to interfere with your prospects receiving your offer, and they can hold onto your piece until such a time that they are ready to view it or will actually need it. They might put it into a file folder labeled "home improvement" and open the file months later. If your artwork is particularly catchy, your piece will be memorable and recalled at a later date (think vibrant colors, a tantalizing recipe, or beautiful artwork).

I remember a designer in Scottsdale who had the exterior of a home sketched by a prominent Canadian artist. She then put this sketch onto a mailer. One lady received it and held onto it for three years. Finally, she called, commenting that she'd saved the piece because it was so beautiful. Now, the Scottsdale designer had been struggling up until that point, and when the call came in, she was considering relocating to Los Angeles for different opportunities. The project value was so large that she decided to stay put and continue her business!

Of course, once you print mailers, you are stuck with that design until you use them all up or do another printing. And printing can be expensive. So can postage, even when using bulk mail rates, especially if you are sending out substantial quantities. Additionally, you must plan for an added delivery time of up to two weeks.

I'm a fan of large-format postcards because they can stand out and be quickly viewed before getting tossed. It's easy to turn a card over to see what is being offered, and inevitably, people do, even if just for a second. Newsletters can also be useful, but they tend to get stacked with other items that can be read at a later date. Warning: that "later" date can be *much* later, like months, or even never (the ultimate "later"). If your target is anything like me, your newsletter may be tossed, unread, even after it has been saved. I will periodically cull the stack and just throw away old newsletters because I decide that too much time has elapsed since receiving them, and I'm still too busy to review them.

On the other hand, if you send something of value or substance, like a heavy brochure, or an invitation to an event (preferably with a hand-written envelope), it will most likely be opened and acted upon quickly—even if that action is throwing it into the trash.

LEARNING BY DOING

It's a balancing act. If you're sending things out in hard copy, printing and postage will determine what finite number you can mail, and usually, the better the piece, the fewer you will be able to afford to send. With e-mail, however, you can send out tens of thousands of messages (most of which will be deleted) at minimal cost.

Whether it is sent electronically or through the post office, direct mail is a good way to test your market, see what generates a response, and keep your name in front of your target audience. Do not expect your first (or second or third) mailing to be on target. It takes time to tailor your pitches, cultivate your lists, and truly understand your audience. Think of each approach as a test at which you will get better and better if you pay attention to the responses. You can also query respondents as to why they chose to respond to a particular offer—or why they didn't. If the offer was an invitation to a reception or tickets to a showcase, you can call people on your list to find out if they received the offer and why they chose not to act on it. Chances are people will give you valuable feedback to incorporate into your next campaign. Your direct mail marketing should constantly be evolving with changing economic conditions. You are never done changing your marketing message and distribution method. There's always more to do and more to learn. And that's the fun of it—you're constantly getting savvier about your market and your clients.

Chapter 6: THE INITIAL INTERVIEW ... AND BEYOND

❖

The initial interview is as much about setting appropriate expectations for your future interactions as it is about determining if you are the right fit for a particular client or project. Here is your chance to set the tone for future communications and give silent instructions about how you want to be treated. This is when you tell a client how much you value your time and ideas—or not. In fact, the initial interview is so vital that I consider this chapter the most important part of this book. You need to pay particular attention to it if you have ever uttered the words, "My clients take advantage of my time." My response to that is, "There are no victims, only volunteers."

As soon as you have first contact with a prospect, or anyone for that matter, whether it is by phone, in person, or electronically, you should subtly impart how you want to be treated. You need to show that you value your time by setting boundaries around your availability and by insisting on appropriate compensation. Be sure to maintain client control; you are interviewing them as much as they are interviewing you.

SETTING BOUNDARIES

So, let's start at the beginning. Suppose a prospect calls you out of the blue. (Actually, this is not the *very* beginning, and it's unlikely that it's really out of the blue; your client has probably called because of your skills at networking and marketing yourself, as we have discussed.) Unless you are working on deadline, you can always take five or ten minutes for a quick, impromptu chat. You might say something like, "Hey, great to hear from you!" and hear what they have to say. After five or ten minutes, you should say something like, "I'd like to know more about this. We should set a time to continue the conversation. When is good for you?" and schedule a time for a longer conversation—even if it's later that same day. The message is that you are busy and organized and your time needs to be pre-arranged. The result is that the other person will never expect you to drop everything and be at their beck and call.

Tell your prospect that you will set aside thirty minutes to speak with them at the scheduled time. Emphasize that there will be no charge for this time while you ask questions about their project and explain your services.

By directing the agenda this way, you are telling them what to expect from your next talk. Anything that falls out of the two areas you mentioned will cost money; your services come at a price. Note that at this point, you have not discussed how much your future work together might cost. How can you? You still don't know much about the project and may never actually bid on it. It's quite possible that the half-hour conversation (which amounts to a telephone screening) will eliminate the need to meet face to face. You may see that this isn't the project for you, and you will have saved time and energy by not having left your office for a meeting. On the other hand, during the telephone screening, you might find the project to be very appealing, and in that case, your next move is to schedule an in-person interview.

PREPARING FOR THE INITIAL INTERVIEW

I recommend scheduling the initial interview at least a week from the initial contact. This establishes the fact that you are busy with other clients and allows you time to send advance materials to the prospect. Include a cover letter outlining the design process and a sample of your letter of agreement, preferably in a neat marketing folder—the goal is to establish your professionalism in everything that you do. An hour is sufficient time for an initial interview, unless the project is particularly large and the walk-through takes a significant amount of time. Be sure to have at least thirty minutes or so to sit down with prospect and have some quality time together. You will constantly lead the conversation by asking questions and keeping prospects focused when they linger too long or talk about irrelevant issues.

For the initial interview, pay particular attention to the following.

ATTIRE

Dress professionally—but not exquisitely. You don't want to outshine your client, nor do you want to indicate that you are a lavish spender. Conversely, you don't want to be too casual, unless the interview takes place at a construction site.

EYE CONTACT

Be sure to look your prospect in the eye as often as you can. Anyone who looks away a lot comes off as uncomfortable or dishonest. This may not be true in other countries or cultures, but it is certainly true in these United States.

Handshake

Whether your client is a man or a woman, reach out and firmly grasp the other person's hand and give it a pump or two. When departing, particularly if you like them and want the project, don't be afraid to use both hands when reaching out. This warm gesture might make a difference. One of my designer-clients failed to get a certain job. I called the prospect, on my client's behalf, to find out why she was not awarded the project. The prospect commented on two things. One, the designer gave a "limp" handshake. Two, she neglected to answer direct questions about pricing. Interestingly, the handshake was mentioned first.

Questions, Questions

During the initial interview, you should be asking most of the questions. This helps you maintain control. Here is a sample list of questions you can ask, whether you are meeting in person or speaking on the phone.

1. What do you want from an interior designer? The goal here is to listen to what the client wants and then set appropriate expectations.

2. Which shelter magazines do you enjoy looking at? Try to elicit information regarding their taste and their price-point: is it *Better Homes & Gardens* or *Architectural Digest?* If they don't read any, ask them to buy a few and put Post-It Notes on the rooms they like. This gives you a psychological advantage because they are doing the things you want and working with you even before they've engaged you.

3. Do you like the way your home is laid out now? What don't you like about the arrangement? Why? What would you like to see differently? Answers to these questions will help you determine their lifestyle and learn about existing problems.

4. Who else will be working on the project (architects, tradespeople, children)? There could be other people that the client has promised to work with or the inevitable friend who is an expert at everything but doesn't actually do anything for a living. Has anyone else been hired? Make sure your project will not be hindered by existing commitments—or at the very least, find out about those commitments before you start the project.

5. What is the project timeline? When would they like to begin and end? Are there any special events (i.e., a wedding or birthday) for which it must be completed? This is the best time to align expectations on delivery. If you know in advance that something is not realistic, inform them and educate them about the process.

6. Do they have a figure in mind for the rough budget? (Of course they do.) Even the richest people have an idea of what they are willing to spend. Unless they write you a blank check, know your limits. Explain the steps needed to arrive at a budget and let them know that determining an accurate budget is part of the design process—for which they will pay.

7. Assuming they are ready to make a decision today, is there any reason they would not hire you? If you want the project, ask for it, but save this for the very end of your interview if you think it has gone well.

DURING THE INTERVIEW

About a half-hour into the interview, I recommend performing a self-check-in. Pause and see if you have covered the fundamental questions. Don't be shy about reminding them that you have only thirty minutes left, and there some questions you still need to ask. You really do need to be a taskmaster, since that's what they'll be (prospectively) paying you for. And you thought you were just a designer. Well, any designer must also be a taskmaster, because the ability to manage others—vendors, workmen, clients—is crucial to success.

If your initial interview is in person, you may want to show the prospect an existing client binder to demonstrate how you work, and how well organized you are. A good project binder contains the contract, client meeting notes, drawings, proposals, purchase orders, invoices, and anything else germane to a project. Showing a binder to a potential client allows them to grasp the design process in all its complexity. Beautiful outcomes don't just happen. The existing client binder (from which you've removed all confidential material, such as the client's name and address) can help convince the prospect that they need to hire a design professional—you in particular, because you are so organized.

Here are some other things to bear in mind during the initial interview. When your prospect asks, "How much will this cost?" your answer is never merely, "I don't know." That may be just what you feel, but this is no time for candor. A better response would be something like, "Project costs are determined by client selections, and I will offer you options within an established range." You can give them an example of what it might cost to furnish a single room, using a range of prices based on quality of materials, delivery times, and other factors. The point here is to educate the client about the availability of options and your role in helping them make selections. Discuss fee structure: hourly design fee or flat fee? (More on this in chapter 7.) Discuss what must be covered, including hourly drafting fees, hourly travel fees, designer's markup (which covers fees for running the project, ordering, tracking, etc.), and anything else they may not know about. Not even the most spontaneous person likes to look at a bill and be surprised.

When meeting in person and presenting your portfolio, explain that the rooms you are showing represent someone else's taste, not theirs and not necessarily yours. You are just the interpreter of your clients' ideas. Different needs, different canvas, different outcomes.

Don't let your prospect be daunted by distance. Say you live in New York City and your prospect lives in Albany. If they pose objections to working with an out-of-area designer who must travel some distance to the project site, tell them, "I am closer to the sources, which translates into cost savings for you." This is a perfect opportunity to explain the process of design. Tell them that through careful planning, you can limit the number of site visits and the money they will have to pay for your travel time.

1. Consider having the initial interview take place in a completed space you have designed. Not only does this show how well you get on with your clients, but it allows you to show your general skill without sharing specific ideas about the future project. You are taking your potential clients out of their space and showing them someone else's. Don't presuppose that a client is not willing to travel to view a project. I know a designer in northern California who was concerned about the distance a prospect would have to travel to view one of her projects and opted for something closer, less than an hour's drive away. Unfortunately, the project she selected was not consistent with the client's expectations, nor did it demonstrate her capacity to meet the client's needs. The project was awarded to another designer for reasons that were entirely avoidable. If only the designer had shown the right project, which was further away, she might have gotten the job.

2. If the initial interview takes a turn toward the conceptualization stage of the design process, you should indicate that the discussion is beyond the scope of this meeting and ask for a fee at that point.

Don't Give It Away

Your prospects know something about what they need. Your role is to help them clarify their needs so you can provide them with solutions. During the initial interview you should explain the services you can provide and outline your process and timeline, without giving any actual ideas. They get those once they've paid for an initial consultation.

If you don't get a project after the initial interview, try to find out why. Learn about your strengths and weaknesses. Remember: You don't want every project that comes your way. Your skills and the project should match. If you are a fast designer, then you will want to turn down a project that involves a person who is indecisive and insists on a fixed fee. Later on, you may be glad you weren't chosen to design that 15,000-square-foot mansion, because you know in your heart that you are happier with smaller projects that focus on décor and do not involve major renovation.

Heaven and Hell

Every designer has stories about the "interview from hell"—and the one from heaven! Here is one of each from my friend Helene Lotto.

Funny but true! Bad interview: I walked into a home, and the prospect bolted the door behind me and removed the key. I began to get nervous. She wore a pitch black wig and looked like Vampira. As we walked through the house, I saw cat feces everywhere. When we got to her bedroom, there was sand in the bed—along with a beautiful young lover. (By the way, the prospect is a famous and well-published New York psychiatrist.) She wanted to hire me, but that house was so freaky, I politely declined.

Good interview: I was referred by an architect, walked into the interview, and spent thirty minutes going over the project with the client and his mother. I was hired then and there, with a $500,000 budget and fees. Those were the days... just a few years back.

Initial Consultation

After the initial interview comes the initial consultation. There is a significant distinction between them: you are paid for the initial consultation. I know of many designers who do not conduct on-site interviews per se, but who charge initial consultation fees. They figure that once they leave their offices, they are investing time—for which they should be paid. Depending upon the amount of business you have, this might be a viable option. The busier you are, the easier it is to call the shots.

I recommend that your initial consultation fee be a multiple of your usual hourly rate, perhaps three to five times the price per hour. This will give you a range of $500 to $1,000 for the first consultation, which should last no more than two hours. While this may seem like a lot of money to some of you, just remember that it represents all of your professional experience, both inside and outside the industry. I maintain that you have the ability to give your clients more ideas in that time then they can possibly execute and that a standard hourly fee is not representative of the value of your ideas. You do not need a contract for this consultation; there is no further commitment on either part, and you should request your check in advance or upon your arrival. This, too, sets an expectation for your client: you expect to be paid prior to delivery of services—not after, and not when and if they feel like it. In fact, I would suggest that you always discuss invoicing matters before design matters so that your clients are conditioned to have their checkbooks at the ready.

Depending upon the size of a project, a certain amount of upfront money may be required as part of due diligence, even if a project does not move forward. Clients may pay for design fees to review architectural plans, travel expenses for a site visit, fees to conduct feasibility studies, and anything else that allows them to have an accurate picture of the overall expenses that might be required to have their vision become reality. Design is a luxury service and not an exact science. Its outcome is not always predictable. If clients are not willing to invest money on the front end, do not assume that they will do so on the back end.

A designer walks a fine line in addressing matters of cost and overall budget during an interview. While you should not be expected to give firm numbers for a project, it is reasonable to offer ballpark estimates, providing ranges of cost when a client asks. You do not need to give them any ideas, but you can say that a new kitchen the size of their existing one may run $50k to $75k. I think this demonstrates your grasp of the situation and allows you to gauge their reactions to the numbers you provide. Naturally, if they seem surprised at a price you give, it's fine to give a bit of a breakdown, explaining the process that would go into a kitchen—design fees, product, labor, etc. I also think that you can cheerfully offer less expensive alternatives, even if they are not through your firm. Here, you are acting from goodwill and as a resource. Ultimately, the more informative you are, the more trustworthy you become, and later on, perhaps, you will be their designer of choice, if one is appropriate. Remember, you are a salesperson whose job is to provide the necessary information for the buyer to make a decision. A good salesperson knows that you do not try to "pitch" clients—you inform and guide them, letting them make the best choices for themselves.

THE ART OF SELLING

I'm sure that some of you are aghast at the last paragraph's suggestion that you are a salesperson. Yes, you are a trained design professional, an artist, a project manager, a taskmaster, etc. But as is any entrepreneur, you are also a salesperson, and you have the responsibility to educate your clients. In order to sell your services, the services of your vendors, and all of the lovely products with which you like to work, you need to be well versed in the art of selling. Here are some helpful concepts to help facilitate this process.

CONVICTION

If you don't fully understand your product, neither will your client. You must be well versed in all aspects of construction, fabrication, materials, labor, delivery methods, and finishes, anything that is germane to a product or service that you wish to sell. You have to speak with conviction about everything so that a client will be confident and relaxed with you. In order to do this, you must understand how everything works, information that can be obtained directly from the manufacturers, showrooms, and tradespeople.

Attention

First, listen to your client, then question, and then provide solutions—but hold off on solutions until you have a signed agreement. You really need to listen to what is being said, and you always need to ask, "Why?" What they say is less important than the reasons behind their statements. All too often, people will instinctively offer their own solutions, telling you what they think they need in the form of a "want." You, on the other hand, are the expert who may very well see different (and often more appropriate) solutions to their needs. Once you explain your reasoning, their "wants" may change to something entirely different. This can only be done by your asking, "Why," and making sure that you fully understand the underlying problems. Take nothing for granted. They may not have even identified their most important need.

For instance, designers often approach me to help them grow their business. They will often say, "I need help with marketing." Upon questioning, I learn that what they really need is to charge more for the very good clients they already attract. In addition, they might also need to save money on their office expenditures. They don't need more clients; they just need to operate differently. This is the kind of thing you learn by questioning and really listening to answers. Think of yourself as a doctor, taking a medical history. You are both actively engaged in a dynamic process, and your would-be client has become an active participant rather than a passive prospect.

Features and Benefits

Products and services are purchased for the function performed. In other words, how something benefits the buyer provides the motivation for obtaining it. You need to explain the features (i.e., an extendable faucet arm) and the benefits (for example, the ability to cover more sink area and thoroughly wash vegetables) in order to highlight the value of that item. If you don't explain what something does and why it is useful, then

MARKETING INTERIOR DESIGN

you can expect there to be a price challenge on that item. People will spend money on things they desire, as long as they understand them.

EMOTIONAL BUYING WITH LOGICAL SUPPORT

Don't forget that purchases are made for emotional reasons. However, long after a purchase is made and the emotion has dissipated, logic should support the original buying decision. You may buy a house because you've fallen in love with it, but six months later, you will have to remind yourself that you selected a home with a ninety-minute commute so that you could afford the payments, enroll your kids in a great school system, and live a quieter life on the weekends. The same holds true with small-ticket items. Whether you are selling a lamp or the service of a painting contractor, you need to know the details in order to support the logic, which will come into play at some point in time.

OBJECTIONS

Don't take a simple "no" for an answer. "No" often means they do not "know" enough. It probably means they do not have enough information to make an informed decision. At this point, you should respectfully say something like, "I understand that you have your reasons for saying no. If you explain them to me, it will help me fine-tune future selections I present to you." Continue your probing questions to make sure that you have in fact answered all of their objections, and fully describe what you are selling. Then, see if the answer is still the same. It is not unusual to effect a change of heart (or is it mind?).

APPROVAL

Whose approval matters to the customer? Almost everyone turns to another person for advice, no matter how tangential, at some point during a project. It is imperative that you figure out who this person is so that you can either get them involved in the process in advance or meet them and tailor your remarks to them as well. I know that it can be hard to suss out these behind-the-scenes characters, but it will save you time in the long run. I know a career woman in her mid-fifties, recently widowed, who embarked on a design project. She had three sons in their twenties who took it upon themselves to make sure mom wasn't being ripped off. Here was a bright woman who decided that the designer should present findings to the family "committee" in order to placate the boys. (I got the feeling the boys were keeping an eye on their inheritance.) While you definitely cannot change the committee, you can explain to the client how additional changes and shopping can drive the price higher. You never want to deny service, but you don't want to be afraid to charge more, if needed.

SELECTION

A final note on the selling process: decisions are made by comparison. You need to provide relevant choices so a client can know that all options have been explored. This does not mean presenting a sofa for $1,000, one for $5,000, and one for $12,000. You should establish a range and then stay within it, with price variations of perhaps 20 to 30 percent. Or, show items that have similar pricing but offer different features. If you have a favorite item, present that last, showing the less desirable options first. And remember to find out the reasons why something is not liked before continuing your hunt. Sometimes people come to a situation just wanting to see options, and lots of them, because shopping is what you do. Not true: your job is to cull the most appropriate selections from the myriad alternatives and present your top picks—usually three. However, if you have a client who insists on seeing twenty items for each one she chooses, make sure you are billing on an hourly basis. Remember, nothing stimulates a client decision more effectively than a ticking billing clock.

Chapter 7: WHAT ARE YOU WORTH?

———————————— ✥ ————————————

Determining the value of your work can be tricky. You have one idea about what you are worth and your prospective client probably has another. In recent negotiations for design firms, I had two people say that while they valued the service the designers were providing and wanted them to make a profit, it was only at a certain amount, an amount my clients thought was too low. Your worth and your clients' estimation of your worth are two values that have to match. This is where the fun begins!

You may be thinking, *fun*?! You may feel more uncertain about negotiating a deal than about any other aspect of design work. After reading this chapter, however, you will feel much more confident reaching a mutually satisfactory price point—and may even come to enjoy the negotiations. Ultimately, there are numerous ways you can charge for your time, and finding the correct combination to present to your client is always a challenge. Finding the particular combination that makes your client comfortable is your ultimate goal. For clients who have worked with a professional before, you might ask them how they were charged by their previous designer and if that was a comfortable method for them. There is no point in trying to force a pricing method on them when it makes them uneasy.

What are you, the designer, selling? You are selling your time and your ideas.

YOUR TIME

If you thoroughly understand the scope of services requested by a client, then you can probably gauge how long it will take to do your portion of the deliverables. Remember, you can only gauge what you have direct control over. This includes creation of design plans, including color schemes, interior finishes, wall coverings, floor coverings, ceiling treatments, lighting and window treatments, layouts showing locations of movable furniture and furnishings, and as needed, recommendations for cabinet work, interior built-ins, and other interior decorative details. You might also need to include the time you will spend in unaccompanied shopping for a client, drafting, etc. Other elements involve other people, including site meetings with contractors and sub-contractors, client meetings, shopping with clients, problems with orders, and other vendor matters. These are basically beyond your control and can last much longer than you anticipate. Nonetheless, you should do the best you can to estimate the length of time it will take you to meet with the other people involved. Add this number to the hours you need to do your own work. We'll call this total X.

YOUR IDEAS AND YOUR HOURLY RATE

Here are some questions you might ponder in determining either an hourly rate or what percentage of the budget you will charge: What are your ideas worth? How good a designer do you think you are? How long have you been in business? How challenging are the design problems facing you on the project? How enthusiastic are you about the solutions you have in mind? What does the competition charge?

If you are based in Los Angeles or New York and have a great reputation, you may ask for $200 plus an hour. If you are in Cleveland, OH and are of the same ilk, you might be hard pressed to get $150 an hour. This is one of the reasons why I do not advocate working on an hourly fee alone—there are too many published rates out there that skew values down and make it too easy for a client to compare a few proposals and just go with the least expensive on paper.

We'll call your hourly rate Y, be it $125 or $250.

Once again, you are selling time and ideas, and perception plays an important role in determining what to ask for. If you use the hourly rate as a multiplier (Y) and multiply it by the estimated number of hours you think you will need in order to create and demonstrate the design (X), you are close to arriving at the design fee.

THE Z FACTOR

Next, factor in another multiplier, Z, which will be anywhere from 3-6, depending upon your level of experience and the difficulty you expect to face with the design solution. The purpose of the Z factor is to provide you with a premium for your time, since it is acknowledged in the industry that an hourly rate alone is not sufficient compensation for design services. The Z factor is the difference between making a living (keeping the lights turned on in your office) and making serious money (saving for a retirement). What will your Z factor be?

- For basic décor such as color schemes, flooring, window treatments, and furniture, your factor might be three. This would be for the design only.

- For basic décor with more complexity, such as built-in furniture or a particularly large room, your factor might be four. Again, this is just for design.

- For kitchens and bathrooms, your factor might be five.

- For new construction and the specifications needed to keep a project on schedule with multiple vendors, your factor might be six or higher.

Your fee will be X (estimated hours) × Y (your hourly rate) × Z (level of difficulty).

Example: 10 hours × $125/hr × 3 (more living room furnishings, color palette, window treatments) = $3,750 for the room. This would be what you would calculate for a design fee.

THE FIXED FEE

You may decide that a fixed fee is more appropriate for the project. A fixed fee is exactly that. It remains the same, despite how many or how few furnishings the client buys. Many clients and designers are comfortable with the fixed fee because at the end there are no surprises. Clients like an "all in" number that accounts for all of your time spent designing, shopping, observing—everything. The designer may find that she is putting more hours into the project than first anticipated, but she also knows that proper compensation doesn't depend on the client spending lavishly on furnishings.

When discussing your fixed fee with your client, you should not indicate the specifics of how you arrived at it. Clients do not need to know your hourly rate, nor do they need to know about the Z factor, which might puzzle them. They do need to know that this is what you have charged for similar jobs. They might need to be reminded that your fee is not based just on time but on the scope of your services and on your experience. They may be relieved to know that this is a set price—that this is what you would charge for similar projects, and you are agreeing to the scope of services at a set price. While you yourself will be keenly aware of the time it will take you to do this, you do not want to be on the clock as far as the client is concerned. You don't want them checking on your hours or calculating how much you are charging per hour. You are a design professional, and as such, you do not punch a clock.

What is important to remember and to discuss with your client is that the fixed fee is probably the most expensive way for a client to pay for services. The reality is that there is no crystal ball with design, and the longer and more involved a project is, the less a design professional knows how long it will take or the exact outcome. More importantly, it is impossible to provide for every eventuality of a project without overestimating the time needed for a project.

With the client who prefers a fixed fee, you can either use the metrics suggested above (X times Y times Z) or you can add your design fee, and your commission on the estimated budget, and then add 25 percent on top of that figure. The project scope could change (often referred to as "project creep"), there may be vendor problems, and the client could be indecisive—all of these factors can lengthen the time needed to get the project done. You must allow for this eventuality, and that is the risk the client takes—paying more than actual time needed. You, too, take some risk. When you commit to a figure, the client will expect you to live with it as long as the project doesn't expand at the client's request (designing for greater square footage, for instance). My hope is that with an inflated premium (that additional 25 percent), your risk is minimal.

DESIGN V. IMPLEMENTATION

It's important not to confuse the work that you do on the design side with that on the implementation side. The creative is different from the execution, and either can be complicated and time consuming. Moreover, a client can choose to only engage you for one service or the other, in which case design and implementation must be separated.

THE INITIAL CONSULTATION, REVISITED

Sometimes, prior to hiring you, the client may ask you to give specific examples of your ideas for their project. Sometimes they are in a rush, or have architectural plans that need to be reviewed in order for a contractor to proceed with work, and they just need some general guidelines or feedback. And this is okay. As discussed in the previous chapter, you can charge an initial consultation fee that is the equivalent of three to five times your hourly rate. For instance, I think $500 to $1,000 is appropriate for an initial consultation, since it is likely that you will answer many questions, solve numerous problems, and provide very important direction, all in the course of one to two hours. It is possible that the client may not ask you back for a variety of reasons, the least likely of which is the quality of your ideas, the most likely of which is the budget and a prior commitment to an architect. So, you want to be sure you are adequately compensated up front.

You should be prepared to ask for an initial consultation fee on the spot when an interview turns into a consultation or if the client is pushing an interview in that direction. Remember, the best way to demonstrate the quality of your ideas is with past examples of your work—not future creativity—so pull out that portfolio. However, if the client agrees to pay you for your thoughts about his project, then you can freely share them and know that you will receive appropriate compensation.

Your initial consultation allows the client an introduction to your work without a full commitment. This provides a way to ease a client into working with you.

THE RECORDING ARTIST

In a recent negotiation between a designer and a major recording artist, the husband told me upfront that he did not want hourly charges because he claimed there was no way for him to know if the time was spent shopping for multiple clients. This client was uncomfortable because he could not audit the time spent and trust that the time charged was legitimate. He was, however, comfortable with paying the designer a percentage of the goods specified for the project: the furnishings, wall coverings, window treatments, and floor coverings that would be bought. This is called "cost-plus," and until recently, this was the most common way of determining a design fee. Naturally, the percentage the husband wanted to pay was 20 percent instead of the 35 percent that my client, the designer, normally charges. There was also the matter of design versus implementation. So, we narrowed down the options and worked on bridging the gap.

The next step and perhaps the most crucial part of the negotiation included listening to the client's perception of the services the designer would provide. I heard a few points with which I did not agree and countered them right away. The client stated that he and his wife pretty much knew what they wanted to have done in the house. I quietly told him that clients frequently end up getting excited about the designer's suggestions and completely forget what they initially have in mind. (Of course, this is not always the case and can be a problem if the client fails to embrace the advice that is being paid for.)

The recording artist and her husband had already engaged a contractor and said that the designer would "only need to provide colors" for the remodeling being done. I know that during a project, designers are always asked to provide more input, not less. I also thought that the aggressive timeline that the contractor was using wasn't realistic; construction usually takes longer than anticipated. I expressed my concerns about this to the client, and while I did not change his mind, at least I had the issues on the table. These sorts of discussions are important, even if they are not initially resolved.

I BEG TO DISAGREE

Sometimes in the course of negotiation, a client won't respond at all to one point or another. I take this as agreement with what I have said. But this goes both ways: if what the client suggests is not to your liking, it is up to you to question and modify it.

I realize that this disagreeing with a prospective client so early in the game may be uncomfortable for many designers, but it is often necessary. Once something is discussed, it becomes the new rule. In this case, the client said that his position "wasn't about money," and that he just wanted to pay a "fair" price for things. I laughingly said that of course it was about money, and informed him that he needed to understand how designers earn their fees. I discussed the design phase and the fact that we need to think of different ways to demonstrate aesthetic while coming up with creative solutions to stay within budget. If we charge them only a percentage of the product, then we would be required to sell them furniture in order to make money, whereas if we assess a design fee upfront, the creative end is paid for and no furniture sales are required for compensation. The furniture sales would be handled separately, in addition to services like drafting, painting, and flooring, with a management fee to cover the time needed to manage those aspects. If we charge more upfront for the design, we can charge less on the back end for the implementation.

Other Factors

There were additional factors to consider. As mentioned, the client is a very high-profile recording artist. Doing the project was important for the firm; having the work included in a portfolio was a valuable plus, with the possibility of publicity yet another bonus.

There is always one more factor to consider: cash in the bank (CIB), meaning whether the firm needs the cash now or it can afford to say no to the project. In this instance, the firm had an "opening" in its schedule (read: really needed CIB) and wanted the project for multiple reasons, so this influenced the negotiation.

Presenting Dual Scenarios

We presented two scenarios for the client to consider. The first option was a fixed fee of 27.5 percent of what the project would cost. This included both products and services. (Remember, initially, the client wanted to pay 20 percent and we wanted to get 35 percent, so we split the difference.) This 27.5 percent would be in place for a period of four months. The time constraint is critical because you do not want to be offering your ideas for an open-ended period—the client can keep asking for more and more of your time and be very picky. Also, this design fee deadline is not the same as the overall contract, which we entered for one year. So our agreement had two timeframes in it.

The second option was an hourly rate for design with a reduced management fee on implementation: 20 percent instead of 27.5 percent. This gave the clients the option to pay for design services separately—which would save them money if they were quick in making choices—and then paying less for the implementation, saving more money the more they spent at a lower management fee. In this case, the client estimated there would be a $400,000 budget and selected the first option, a fixed percentage of the entire budget. However, if the client had planned on spending significantly more, say $600,000, then the second option could have been the better of the two.

THE RELUCTANT BANKER

Another negotiation involved a banker and the remodel of his weekend property. The banker was referred to the designer by a trader friend whose property he greatly admired. The designer had executed a design for the trader with the project totaling $500,000. This included built-in furniture and custom-created pieces, as well as some remodeling of the kitchen and bathrooms. The project had been completed two years earlier and the designer had received a flat 25 percent cost-plus from the trader for all products and services. This amounted to $125,000—not chicken feed!

However, by the time the banker wanted to hire him, the designer had more experience and felt that this fee was too low, considering the amount of time he'd put into the house. He vowed that his next project would be more favorably priced. (This is where I came in!)

Needless to say, the trader had talked to the banker, so the banker knew about the fee for the previous project. So, my first conversation with the banker was about designers setting prices that are appropriate for specific projects and during specific time periods. Since the other project was two years old, we reserved the right to raise our prices.

Next, there was the matter of budget, since the banker wanted to spend about $300,000 and not the $500,000 his friend had spent—although, of course, he wanted similar, if not better results. This actually made my next argument easier, since it takes more creativity to work with less money, more time to research less expensive options, and more time to come up with multiple solutions. In other words, smaller budgets can take as much time or more than larger budgets and therefore require more design-time billing.

My solution was to assess a non-refundable design fee of $20,000 in addition to a mark-up of 35 percent on the product.

This was met with immediate resistance because the banker had paid less for a previous project with another designer (a $5,000 design fee, which was applied to a 15 percent mark-up), was afraid that after paying an upfront fee he would not like the designs, and resented paying 10 percent more on the cost-plus than the trader, who had spent more in total on his house. I discussed this with the designer, and he really wanted to do this job, but not on the banker's terms, so we countered the offer.

In fact, I countered the offer with the banker via phone and e-mail about ten times.

Each time we revised a point of the agreement, the banker analyzed the terms even more carefully and wanted further explanations and guarantees on the design elements, defining and redefining what he would be getting for the up-front fee. This left my client doubting the desirability of the banker as a client. He said, "I'm not sure I even like him anymore!" My job was to explore the situation and help my client make decisions that were favorable to him in the long run.

Now, the banker traveled a great deal for work and would sometimes not respond for over a week. Add this to the fact that my designer client frequently "slept" on things before deciding—and our negotiation dragged on for three months. This actually worked in our favor, however, because the banker realized he was not making the negotiation easy and finally apologized for being unresponsive. He became more communicative. I continued to push our points and not give in. When the banker wanted the designer to have more liability for other vendors' products and services, I flatly refused. I started saying that we needed to "bring this in for a landing" for the benefit of both sides.

The banker finally agreed to a revised offer of $10,000 for a design fee and 25 percent of the cost of all products and services. While this represents only a modest increase from the beginning of our negotiation, it is nonetheless $10,000 more for the designer—less my negotiation fee, of course.

Ironically, at the writing of this book, the banker got a request from his employer to relocate—so we only have a deal if he stays.

PRICING BY THE SQUARE FOOT

Another way to calculate a design fee is to assign a price per square foot of the space that is being designed. This method is frequently used by architects and contractors when they bid their projects. Essentially, you have a multiplier that you use in conjunction with the actual square footage of the space you will work on. I recommend between $5 and $20 per square foot, utilizing the same factors mentioned earlier (experience of the designer, difficulty of the work, location of the house). Five dollars per square foot is appropriate for décor and can rise to twenty dollars or more for new construction.

If you have never charged this way before and think that five dollars is too high, try something a bit lower, but not less than three dollars per square foot. Remember, you have to set the bar of negotiation at a point below which you will not descend. You may need to say no to the project rather than dilute the value of your services and create problems for other designers in the area. You are setting a precedent with your pricing.

PERCENTAGE OF THE BUDGET

Your colleagues in design have yet another method for determining a design fee: charging a percentage based on the overall budget the designer is responsible for. This is relevant when there is construction involved and you will be supervising tradespeople and craftspeople. Depending upon the complexity of the project, you may request a fee of 10 to 20 percent of the budget. This is based on the construction as well and means that you will provide your design concept and oversight of the work being done. The furnishings can be negotiated separately.

THE WINE BAR BROTHERS

When a Los Angeles designer asked me to handle negotiation for a second project with two of his clients, who are brothers, I knew I was in for a treat. The brothers are sharp businessmen and are well versed in commercial ventures. They had already created one very successful wine bar and were now creating another for investment purposes. As was no surprise, they wanted to spend only a little more on the project than they had done on the previous one, which was 40 percent smaller and done a year earlier. And, as should be the case, my client wanted to raise his rates as well.

Our initial foray with the brothers was to request a design fee of $15 per square foot that did not include the purchasing. We understood that the client wanted to place orders on their own through their contractor. When we actually sat down to negotiate in person (after perhaps a month of waiting for permits and waiting for the client to dismiss another designer who had done $15,000 worth of preliminary work), it became apparent that what the client really needed was a full-service designer.

I explained the process and asked if they in fact wanted to be responsible for the intricacies of ordering lighting and if they really wanted to be on-site to make sure that what was ordered was the same as what was being delivered. They quickly saw the error of their thinking and decided that they would be willing to pay for full-service designing.

Unfortunately, even after a thorough explanation of the value-add of full-service, the client was dismayed by the additional cost of this service: about $19 per square foot instead of the $15 per square foot we'd originally told them. As a note to the reader, the design fee was on the high side for negotiation purposes and rather than do a traditional mark-up (which we failed at getting), it was clear that the only way to bring this deal in for a landing was to eliminate variables and find a single number. You see, the clients loved the negotiation process, so it could have gone on indefinitely. Arriving at a fixed fee for the project simplified and expedited the process.

Once we got down to the basic amount of the fixed fee, we then discussed budget so that we could get an idea of what the client was willing to spend, and more importantly, know going into the project whether they were being realistic. They wanted to spend $200,000 for the tenant improvements on the commercial space and for that to include the designer's fee. We immediately said that $250,000 was more accurate—and then the bargaining began.

Normally, my client is not present for negotiations, but in this instance, he was; the four of us were dining at the existing wine bar and restaurant. So, when the appropriate moment arrived, I excused myself and my client to discuss strategy. We decided what was an acceptable number and at what point we would walk from the table ... and walk we did! Well, almost. I did have to say that we were too far off and that I could not let my client take the project for the suggested price of $15 per square foot. The clients were under a sharp deadline and needed to satisfy their landlord and sign a deal in short order, so I knew they needed us. Next, they left the table. This went back and forth a few times. We were finally down to a $2,500 difference, and we prevailed, getting that extra amount for a total of $16.25 per square foot for all services rendered.

Now, before you think that this is too low, we did manage to transfer all check writing to the client for the orders, relieving my client of the burden and liability of placing the orders. We also limited the number of times that the designer would be obliged to meet the clients and established a base-line for hourly work for anything that was above and beyond the scope of services. Finally, we insisted that the permit responsibility remain that of the clients. Given that the clients are repeat customers and will be duplicating the model throughout Los Angeles, this pricing made sense, and my client was very happy!

TIERED PRICING

In happy instances when a project has a furnishings budget in excess of $100,000, it may be reasonable to offer a tiered pricing structure. If you can get a full mark-up of 35 percent for the first $100,000 of furnishings, you can reduce your mark-up by 5 percent for every additional $100,000 in product, thus giving the client a volume discount and the incentive to spend more money. So, the mark-up would be $35,000 on the first $100,000; $30,000 on the next $100,000 increment; and $25,000 on the remaining increments. I do not recommend going below 25 percent, as further discounting suggests that there is "fluff" in your pricing. Nonetheless, you can certainly massage these numbers and arrive at a blend that works for you.

CONFIDENCE

Now that you have read some examples of real-life pricing, you need to go at it on your own. How do you feel about this? If you are not feeling up to the challenge, you need to ask yourself why. Could it be that you have not asked for much in the past and don't feel that you can ask for more now? If this is the case, I can empathize with you.

When I started my career as a consultant I was charging $125 per hour and thought that was good money. But when I started working with my business coach, Ron Charnock, he quickly ran some numbers and informed me that at that rate, I would not be getting rich quickly—or ever! He asked me to double my rate. Naturally, I did not think I was worth it because I did not have the validation of ever having received that rate. I had not thought of myself as a $250 per hour consultant.

So, with trepidation, I approached my next potential client and told her that my hourly rate was $250, and not surprisingly (easy to say now), she agreed to it. My invoice for that forty-five-minute call was $167.50—and I was officially worth $250 per hour. Now, as a word of caution, billing anything at a one-time charge of forty-five minutes, particularly for an initial consultation, is still undervaluing your services. So, while I had gotten myself over the "worth" hurdle, I was still not effectively charging for my services for a quick project. $250 per hour is terrific if you can bill twenty or more hours, but is not worth it for just an hour or two. This is where pricing on initial consultations (as outlined earlier) comes into play. My initial consultation rate is now $1,000 for the first hour.

DON'T LOWER YOUR RATE: SELL LESS SERVICE!

You will not get every prospect that you meet to agree with your rates or initial consultation fees, and this is to be expected. You may find it hard to hold out if you don't have CIB, but it is critical that you don't lower your rate. Instead, just consider selling less of your service. I have sold many half-hour consults for $500, giving my clients much-needed advice with an expense they can afford while still honoring my $1,000 per hour rate. You should use this idea whenever needed. Don't discount your rates; instead, reduce the scope of the service or the time you provide to the client.

Chapter 8: THE CONTRACT: DESIGN AND IMPLEMENTATION

❖

There are two main phases to a project: design (concept) and implementation (execution). While there are certainly other phases, especially with construction, I want you to have a simplified way of organizing your thoughts: ultimately, all items will fall under these two headings. As you learned in the previous chapter, this structure is also helpful when it comes to pricing and making sure that you are being compensated for each service, independent of the other. In the design phase, you outline your creative ideas in a manner your client understands. This may require visual displays that demonstrate colors, shapes, textures, and spatial requirements. In the implementation phase, you actually execute your plan and work with vendors to provide the services and products needed to fulfill your vision. Even if you are hired for both phases, you need to approach each as if you are only doing that phase in order to define your scope of services and be properly compensated.

Everything you and your client agree to should be put in writing to produce a binding document that records your understanding of how a project will proceed. This document protects both designer and client by articulating expectations for both sides. If it is not in writing, you have no way of enforcing it, so leave nothing to chance or goodwill. You can't prove a conversation unless you record it. I will now outline the basic concepts and sections of the letter of agreement (or contract) so that you can prepare one for your next project.

SPECIFYING THE AREA

Specifying the area is the first step to defining the project. It is not sufficient to write the property address alone and think that defines the scope, even if you are doing the entire home. You need to be specific and say which rooms are being completed. If it is a new construction, then put in the estimated square footage of construction. This may be a paragraph; there's no need to be brief. The reason you are being definitive is to put a cap on the services that you may provide, versus having something that is open-ended. If you are only doing the living room and don't so specify, the client could ask that you also decorate the foyer leading into it. This is fine if you are being compensated for it, but not fine if you charged a fixed fee for that room and then were expected to do more. It's entirely possible that after you finish the work you set out to accomplish, you may refuse to take on more, for any number of reasons (an irritating client, prior obligations, vacation plans, etc.). If you've specified the area in your contract, you will have fulfilled your obligation and honored your agreement. And should you decide to continue working for the client, you can re-bid on subsequent phases.

PROJECT DEVELOPMENT AND BUDGET

Specifying the project development is very important because it is the basis for your fees. Describe the steps that will be taken to complete a project, listing point by point what you will do to help the client achieve her vision. Keep in mind that you, not your client, are the expert, and that things you might take for granted during a project may come as a surprise to them. Since you want to be paid for everything you do, go ahead and spell it out. Start at the beginning with intake meetings, measurements and however you conduct a design study. Then, add in shopping and competitive bidding, installation, final accessorizing, and whatever else is called for by the project. This section may be several paragraphs long by the time you are done. Aim to be both succinct and comprehensive.

In part of this section, you will discuss the process used to develop a budget. This is the best way to bring up the subject, since it tends to be a sticky point. More often than not, when queried about budget, a client will respond, "I don't know—I was hoping you would tell me how much I need to spend." This gives you leave to discuss your process, making it clear that determining a budget falls under the process of design. Once the agreement is signed, developing a budget is something you are paid to do. While you can give rough estimates as to the costs of certain items or general expenditures, an actual budget takes time to prepare. It is a reasonable expectation that the client will know roughly what a project will run before they sign an agreement, and they should also know that ultimately, they drive the final budget.

Purchasing

Purchasing tends to be the one section that designers don't omit, since product can be an essential part of a project. In fact, I've seen mini-agreements that only address this one section. However, you are going to be a good businessperson and cover all your bases. You will explain how you go about placing orders and that you will generate written proposals, which will contain complete descriptions of whatever product or service is being ordered. You might attach tear sheets to these proposals to provide a visual representation as well. You will discuss how much of a deposit is required and at what points more money will be requested. You are not required to take 50 percent deposits; this just happens to be the amount required by many vendors. You can decide the appropriate amount for each order. For orders up to $5,000, I recommend asking for 100 percent of the product, sales tax, and delivery, as well as your commission. Paperwork is onerous, and you can save yourself time and money by eliminating the need for a later collection process.

MARK-UP

You also need to address your mark-up or commission in your contract. Historically, designers have generally established a set amount for an entire project, ranging from 20 percent to 40 percent or more. However, there is nothing cast in stone that says it must be done this way. In fact, I suggest that you not specify a percentage, and just leave it open. You could say, "Each proposal will describe the item and the price you need to pay to have it delivered to your home." That leaves you the flexibility to charge more on certain items and less on others. Many firms will double the cost of textiles for their mark-up, while only adding 35 percent to the cost of furniture. Their rationale is that textiles are less expensive and can absorb more commission while furniture, typically much more highly priced, would become prohibitively expensive if a designer were to charge a commission of 100 percent.

What if you have a personal item that you wish to sell to your client—something that has been in your family for generations—that doesn't have a retail price? You could get an estimate from an appraiser or just make up a number—a number that does not have a mark-up per se, but still reflects what you want in exchange for the item. The customer always has a choice in the matter, and it is the final price that counts, not the amount of a commission.

If you do establish a mark-up, remember that it is based on your best net cost, or the price that you obtain an item for. So, regardless of the source of your purchase, be it a trade-only vendor you have used for decades or a retail store in a heavily trafficked mall, you agree to charge clients a set price on top of whatever you negotiate on their behalf. Some designers are concerned that if they purchase something from a retail source and then add a commission to it, their client will end up paying more than the retail price. This is absolutely true. It is important to understand that what they are paying for is the service, the selection, and the placement of an item, in addition to the item itself, and that the retail price is merely a reference point.

I have a favorite analogy that helps explain this. Imagine that you are a chef and that your client is a patron of your restaurant. You can both shop at the same markets for the same ingredients, but only you can masterfully assess and prepare the ingredients, combining them in a pleasing manner for your guest to savor. Moreover, you take the time to shop, clean, cook, and serve this meal to the guests, and that is what they are paying for. Even in the unlikely case that your client has the skills to do this, it is you who has invested the time, and that is time for which you must be paid. To extend the restaurant metaphor still further, you are right to expect your just desserts.

PROTECTING YOURSELF

There is a phenomenon unique to design. After clients start working with interior designers, they feel more confident about their own taste and design abilities and decide that they can make purchases on their own. Naturally, it becomes easier after a designer has educated them and shown them what to look for. And it is odd how the purchases they make are sometimes exactly what you have shown them during your shopping forays. While you can't prevent this from happening, you can certainly discourage outside shopping with language like the following: "Any purchases made during the course of this project, whether or not purchased by our firm, will be included in the overall budget on which our fees are based."

The main purpose of this sentence is to set an appropriate expectation for the entire project. You can explain that once you begin showing them design inspirations, you expect to execute the purchases related to your ideas. However, to be reasonable, you should ask if they have certain pieces that they want to source themselves or if they have a shopping trip planned that you can coordinate together. If either of these is the case, you can consider a modified process in which they send you images for approval, allowing you to make sure that size and color work for the scheme that you have devised, and you can charge a lower percentage on those pieces. This way, the client is happy, you have been reasonable, and you have minimized a potential source of conflict.

If you have a provision in place to collect your commission on items your client buys, then you can legitimately invoice them for the commission, based on a price that you know or can reasonably estimate from similar products. If the client refuses to pay this invoice, then you can deduct it from the retainer money you have on account and are (wisely) holding until the end of the project, for just such circumstances. (Retainer money is discussed later in this chapter.)

INCLUDABLE ITEMS

Sometimes an architect or contractor may have a contract that provides for commission on items that you plan on specifying as well. Typically, these items include plumbing and lighting fixtures or surface materials, such as tiles and stone slabs. If you anticipate this overlap and know that you are the one doing the creative side and most of the work, then go ahead and draw attention to these specific items. List them in your agreement as "includable items" so that there is absolutely no question that you will be specifying and ordering these items as part of your services. If you only want to specify them and are alright with a reduced commission, you can include that percentage at this point. I think that 15 to 20 percent for specifying (selecting, not purchasing) is reasonable and that the same for ordering is an equitable distribution of profits. Once again, the time to negotiate this is before the project begins. Once a contractor has the house torn up, he or she has the upper hand, since the only thing on which your client is focusing is finishing—not your commission!

BOILERPLATE

Your letter of agreement will continue with additional items, which are often referred to as "boilerplate." Don't be fooled into thinking that boilerplate is unimportant. Quite the reverse is true. Boilerplate implies that every agreement should include these items because they are so important. Following are some key boilerplate items you should include in your agreement.

Small businesses may be staffed by one person and one person only—the sole proprietor. So, if you are a one-person shop, be sure to let your clients know that from time to time, other members of your staff may work on their projects. Writing about this phantom staff protects you in the event that you get a large, new project and need to hire additional help. At that point, it is strategic for you to focus on the creative aspects of the new project, while your (possibly new) staff aids with the execution of the existing project. Since you wisely included language about your staff in your agreement, your current clients have been given proper notice.

Another issue is the work of other vendors you suggest for the project. You should never sign those agreements on behalf of your clients; instead, insist that they sign the agreements directly. Moreover, make sure your contract says that your firm is not responsible for the performance, quality, timely completion or delivery of work, materials, or equipment furnished by the individuals who have signed agreements with you. Interestingly, some designers have questioned this concept, suggesting that it is they who made the recommendation and to whom the client has entrusted the project and it is they who should be held liable. While this is all very noble, it is not a prudent way to run a business. If you wish to be liable, so be it. If not, then protect your interests accordingly. The benefit of being self-employed is being able to run your business as you see fit.

I recommend that site visits, whenever possible, be billed at your usual hourly rate, since one can never predict how long they will take. And don't forget to bill your travel time to all appointments, especially when they are more than thirty minutes from your office. Time away from the office is time away from designing, and all time is billable.

Another important consideration is obtaining written client approval on everything related to the project. This begins with the contract that this chapter covers. I cannot begin to tell you how many times I have heard of designers who take the time to issue a contract to a client and never get the contract signed. They take the deposit check as a sign of acceptance of the agreement, which it is not. Writing a check does not mean that your client agrees to all terms of the contract. Clients can stipulate all kinds of oral agreements at this point, many of which are binding in certain states of the union. I am reminded of the designer who was working on a $10 million renovation in Dallas, and near the end decided to authorize the delivery of $80,000 in furnishings because the client requested he do so and promised to pay the money (but never signed the order). A dispute ensued, and the client changed his mind about the furniture, so the designer was in jeopardy and had to obtain an attorney so he wasn't liable for the balance of the money owed on the furniture. You would think this is a clear-cut breach of contract on the client's side, but even something so seemingly obvious required an attorney's involvement to get the designer off the hook.

Whenever possible, husband and wife should both sign the contract, and that applies to unmarried couples as well. In the event that there is a divorce or a breakup, you will often find that the person who signed the agreement is not the person who has the money.

Sign on the Line

During the course of the project, there will be other times you should request a signature from your client: on proposals for products and services, on contracts with other vendors, on change orders, on visual representations of proposed work, and on architectural plans. And if you miss a signature on something, it's all right to go back before the project ends and have them sign it to ensure that your files are properly annotated. You can have them sign your proposal as well as a tear sheet on the product—and even the fabric sample, while you're at it.

Does this sound obsessive and time consuming? Well, clients can be crazy. I have heard tales of clients placing orders for products and then saying, "That is not what I ordered," even when it was exactly what they ordered. More often than not, one spouse doesn't like the furniture when it is delivered or a trusted friend expresses disapproval and the client decides they just don't like it. Try and imagine how much time and money it will take to defend yourself in a legal action, and then think again about having everything signed.

Stabilizing Cash Flow

Many designers are challenged by the irregularity of cash flow inherent with design projects. They may obtain large fees up front and then not see any more money for six months. Then, they get another injection of cash with the initial order deposits and then not again for several more months. It's hard to run a business when the cash flow is irregular and every month your bills are amazingly on time.

If you are anticipating a project that will last a year or more, it's a good idea to estimate the fees you will earn over the course of the project, amortize that on a monthly basis, and bill your client that figure every month. So, if your estimate is $60,000 in fees for the project over twelve months, ask for a $10,000 deposit and the balance over eleven months, or $4,166 per month.

This will stabilize your cash flow, and you can make adjustments further along the project as estimates become actual and require more money before the project's completion. Make sure that all deposit money on product is collected before merchandise is delivered. It is also good policy to collect most of your money long before you finish your work. It is common practice, unfortunately, not to pay a designer a final invoice on particularly large projects. Often, a client instinctively knows that the designer will not take them to court, and they feel the designer has already made so much money, he or she will just ignore the matter.

Because of this situation, retainers are recommended on all projects.

Retainers

A retainer is money that is collected upfront and is refundable to the client at the end of the project. You will apply any final invoices to it and return the balance to your client. This is different from your design fee, which is also collected upfront, but is nonrefundable. Once you start giving design ideas and direction, the money is yours to keep, even if the plan is not executed. There is also money collected on deposit for product. That is collected the time of an order and, for the most part, is also nonrefundable. The industry shies away from cancellation of custom merchandise since it is usually only salable to the client for whom it was ordered. However, there are certain manufacturers who allow returns with a stocking fee, and that fee is then deducted from the client proceeds. In case of cancellation, you should not forgo your entire commission, if any. Why should you go through the work of placing the order and have your fee be contingent upon the client taking delivery? Insist on a percentage of the commission, say a third, as your restocking fee.

To illustrate the difference between your design fee and retainer, suppose you are charging a design fee of $5,000 to design a room or two. You may also ask for a retainer on potential time you could invest further in project, say $2,500, and therefore request an initial check of $7,500 to commence the project. Remember, the $2,500 is still the client's and is held on account for them and applied to outstanding invoices at the end of the project. Deposits taken for product and services from other vendors will almost always be paid for before delivery and therefore prior to the end of the project.

BEAUTY SHOTS

One thing to include in the contract is permission for you to take, or have a photographer take, pictures of the completed project for your portfolio, etc. If you have not made provisions in your agreement to take images of your product, you may not get a chance to do so. Don't assume that your client will say yes or that they will be happy at the end of the project. Make sure they agree to photography in advance. Persuade them that a photographic record will serve you both well.

And take those pictures early. Try to schedule a photographer on a day immediately following final installation. While I know that this can be a challenge if you have not yet received all the accessories or artwork, take the photos anyway, even if you must do so with product you bring in just for the occasion. This way, you'll have the photos on your timeframe, not your clients'. I have witnessed many situations in which clients dawdle and delay over finishing touches, and the designer loses the chance to capture valuable marketing material. How valuable are these photos? Good question. How much do you think you will make on your next project? You may not get it if you can't demonstrate your best work, so take those pictures as soon as you can.

Litigation

In most cases, when a project is completed, both designer and client are happy. On occasion, though, there are misunderstandings and disagreements, leading to claims for financial recompense. In other words, you may be sued. You may do everything right and still find yourself in legal battle with a client. I was just contacted by a friend of mine from San Francisco who had completed multiple projects for a client. The client decided that he was not happy with the outcome, and has now sued my acquaintance eleven times. While he has not been to court each time, this matter has dragged on for years, and each charge has to be answered, however frivolous or untrue.

It behooves all business people to watch for warning signs and avoid potentially litigious clients. For instance, if you are not the first designer a potential client has worked with in your area, find out what ended the previous relationship. Don't be afraid to ask who the client worked with and why the relationship ended. Then call the designer to verify the story. Out of solidarity, most designers will tell you the truth.

Sometimes a client turns irrational and vengeful without any warning. You can provide for such an eventuality by stipulating that in case of disagreement, you and your client will first try mediation. Mediation allows both sides to address their concerns, to be heard, and to hopefully reach a resolution, in a non-confrontational way and without the need for expensive lawyers. Mediation, however, is non-binding, and either side can change their mind after reaching an agreement.

Or, your contract might stipulate that if you and your client disagree, you both submit to arbitration, which is more formal than mediation and is binding. Arbitration sessions are held outside of the court and are usually presided over by an attorney who is trained as an arbitrator. You are usually represented by your own attorney. While a few states (such as New York) are starting to challenge that arbitration is mandatory if it is in the contract, most states still allow it. (There are chapters of the American Arbitration Association in each of the fifty states that can give you information and referrals.) Arbitration is quicker and less expensive than municipal court, but if it isn't in the contract, you can't insist on it later.

Depending upon the value of your dispute, there is also the option of Small Claims Court which is inexpensive, quick, and binding. However, different cities have different limits, from as low as a $2,500 maximum to a high of $15,000. A $5,000 cap is average. If you choose this option, you will only be able to apply for the maximum amount and will forfeit any claims above that.

SCHEDULING THE PROJECT

When you present the contract to your client, be sure to say how much you look forward to working together. And make sure they know what needs to happen next. You need to get back a signed original of your agreement, so you provide them with two copies, both with your signature, and request one fully executed copy back with the deposit check. They need to know that upon receipt of the signed agreement and deposit, you will schedule their project. Notice that I did not say "begin," since that would imply you are sitting around with nothing to do and can start at a moment's notice. Even if this is the case, they don't need to know this. Scheduling a project reminds them that there is a process to be followed, that there are calendars to watch, and that there are other clients in the world who also require your attention. There is a difference between providing exceptional service and being a welcome mat. I have always liked the expression, "I'm at your service, not at your mercy." Provide the best customer service you can, but at the same time, retain your dignity and self-respect.

While a contract cannot guarantee all of this, it certainly can help create greater fulfillment for you and your client.

Designer-Client Agreement for Residential Project

[Designer's Letterhead]

Date

Ms. Alice Client
123 Main Street
Greenwich, CT 06830

Dear Ms. Client:

We are delighted to have been selected by you for your interior design project (the "Project"). This letter is to set forth the terms under which we will work together.

1. Description. We agree to design the Project in accordance with ❑ the following plan ❑ the plan attached hereto as Schedule A and made part of this agreement.

Project location, including identification of areas, square footage, and likely number of occupants:

_____
_____
_____

Scope of work to be performed:

_____
_____
_____
_____

Scope of work set forth in project phases:

Program plan. We shall consult with you to ascertain your goals, interview the people who will use the space, visit the premises and make measurements, prepare designs and renderings, and offer recommendations for purchases of merchandise and construction (including sample materials, when helpful). Other services we will render during this phase include:

_____
_____
_____
_____

❑ If this box is checked, Designer shall prepare an estimated budget to include in the presentation, but you acknowledge that this budget is subject to change and is not a guarantee on our part with respect to the prices contained therein.

Design documents. After your approval of the presentation, we shall prepare interior architectural drawings for the following areas _____
_____, which, after your further approval, shall be submitted for competitive bids to contractors selected by you after consultation with us. In addition, we shall prepare purchase orders for merchandise and construction for your approval. Other services we will render during this phase include:

_____
_____
_____
_____

Contract reproduced by permission from *Business and Legal Forms for Interior Designers,* © Tad Crawford and Eva Doman Bruck 2001.

Design implementation. We shall visit the Project with the following frequency ⎯⎯⎯⎯⎯⎯⎯⎯⎯ , discuss the status of the work with you, and be available to consult with you with respect to whether what is being delivered or constructed is in conformity with specifications and of suitable quality. However, the quality and supervision of merchandise or construction shall be the responsibility of the suppliers or contractors. Other services we will render during this phase include:

⎯⎯⎯

Services to be rendered by us in addition to those described above:

⎯⎯⎯

2. Schedule. We agree to make our presentation within ⎯⎯⎯ days after the later of the signing of this Agreement or, if you are to provide reference, layouts, measurements, or other materials specified here ⎯⎯⎯⎯⎯⎯⎯⎯⎯⎯ ,

after you have provided this to us.

After approval of the presentation, we shall ❑ make reasonable efforts to progress the Project; or ❑ shall conform to the following schedule: ⎯⎯⎯⎯⎯⎯⎯⎯⎯⎯⎯⎯⎯⎯⎯⎯⎯⎯⎯⎯⎯⎯⎯⎯⎯⎯⎯⎯⎯⎯⎯⎯⎯⎯⎯⎯⎯⎯⎯

based on an intended occupancy date of ⎯⎯⎯⎯⎯⎯⎯⎯⎯⎯⎯⎯⎯⎯⎯⎯⎯⎯⎯⎯⎯⎯⎯⎯⎯⎯⎯⎯ .

You understand that delays by you, suppliers, or contractors may delay performance of our duties, and our time to perform shall be extended if such delays occur. In addition, if we or you are unable to perform any obligations hereunder because of fire or other casualty, strike, act or order of a public authority, act of God, or other cause beyond our or your control, then performance shall be excused during the pendency of such cause.

3. Purchases of merchandise and construction shall be handled in the following manner:
❑ We shall pay for purchases of merchandise, and you shall pay for construction.
❑ We shall commit to purchases of merchandise and construction as your agent, but you shall make payment directly to the suppliers or contractors.
❑ You shall pay for purchases of merchandise and construction.
❑ We shall pay for purchases of merchandise and construction.
❑ Other arrangement ⎯⎯⎯⎯⎯⎯⎯⎯⎯⎯⎯⎯⎯⎯⎯⎯⎯⎯⎯⎯⎯⎯⎯⎯⎯⎯⎯⎯⎯⎯⎯⎯⎯⎯⎯⎯

If we are paying for either merchandise or construction, you shall give advance approvals by signing written authorizations. You shall pay us in full for lighting fixtures, fabrics, wallpaper, plants, flatware, crystal, linen, china, and other household items, pay a deposit of ⎯⎯ percent for other merchandise; and pay a deposit of ⎯⎯ percent for construction. You understand that we shall not place any order until after receipt of the signed approval with appropriate payment. Once we place such an order, it cannot be cancelled by you. If a deposit has been made, the full balance due shall be paid by you prior to delivery, installation, or completion of construction.

If we are acting as your agent, you shall approve all purchases of merchandise or construction by signing a written authorization.

We shall prepare purchase orders for purchases of merchandise or construction and shall advise you as to acceptability, but shall have no liability for the lateness, malfeasance, negligence, or failure of suppliers or contractors to perform their responsibilities and duties. In the event that, after your approval for purchases of merchandise or construction, changed circumstances cause an increase in price or other change with respect to any such purchases of merchandise or construction, we shall notify you in writing, but shall bear no liability with respect to the changed circumstances, and you shall be fully responsible with respect to the purchases of merchandise or construction. We make no warranties or guarantees as to merchandise or construction, including but not limited to fading, wear, or latent defects, but will assign to you any rights we may have against suppliers or contractors, and you may pursue claims against such suppliers or contractors at your expense.

If you pay directly for purchases of merchandise or construction, you shall make certain that we receive copies of all invoices.

You shall be responsible for the payment of sales tax, packing, shipping, and any related charges on such purchases of merchandise or construction.

4. Approvals. On our request, you shall approve plans, drawings, renderings, purchase orders, and similar documents by returning a signed copy of each such document or a signed authorization referencing such documents to us.

5. Your Responsibilities. You shall cooperate throughout the Project by promptly providing us with necessary information; arranging any interviews that may be needed; making access available to the project site; giving prompt attention to documents to review and requested approvals; facilitating communications between us and other professionals, such as architects and engineers whom you have retained; and, if necessary, designating the following person _____ to act as liaison with us. If you are to provide specifications, floor plans, surveys, drawings, or related information, this shall be at your expense, and we shall be held harmless for relying on the accuracy of what you have provided. If at any time you have knowledge of a deviation from specifications or other problem with the Project, you shall promptly give notice in writing to us. You shall be responsible for receiving, inspecting, and storing all deliveries, except that we shall assist in this as follows:

_____
_____
_____

6. Remuneration. You agree to pay us on the following basis, as selected by a check mark in the appropriate box or boxes:

❑ Retail/list price plus a percentage of construction costs. We shall purchase merchandise at retail/list price and shall be compensated through the discount customarily allowed designers from such retail/list prices. If construction is required, we shall be paid a markup of ____ percent of construction expenditures. You shall pay us a nonrefundable retainer of $____ on the signing of this Agreement, which retainer shall be applied to reduce the last payments due to us from you or, if insufficient purchases of merchandise and construction are made for the retainer to be so applied, shall be retained as a design fee.

❑ Flat fee plus a percentage of costs. Our compensation shall be a nonrefundable design fee of $____, paid by you on the signing of this Agreement, plus an additional markup of ____ percent of the expenditures for merchandise and ____ percent of the expenditures for construction, except that the following budget items shall not be included in this calculation:

_____
_____
_____

Regardless of whether payment is made by us or you, all purchases of merchandise and construction for the Project shall be included for the purpose of computing remuneration due us, except for the following exclusions:

_____
_____
_____

In addition, you may append to this Agreement a list of items owned by you prior to commencement of the Project and use these items without any additional fee being charged by us.

❑ If an Estimated Budget is required by you, an additional fee of $____ shall be charged for its preparation.

In the event that design services beyond the scope of work for this Project are requested by you and we are able to accommodate your request, we shall bill for such additional services as follows:

_____
_____
_____

7. Revisions. During the development of the Project, we shall make a reasonable amount of revisions requested by you without additional charge, but if the revisions are requested after approvals by you, an additional fee shall be charged as follows:

_____
_____

8. Expenses. In addition to the payments pursuant to paragraphs 6 and 7, you agree to reimburse us for all expenses connected to the Project, including but not limited to messengers, long-distance telephone calls, overnight deliveries, and local travel expenses. These expenses shall be marked up ____ percent by us when billed to you. In the event that travel beyond the local area is required, the expenses for this travel shall be billed as follows:

_____

_____

At the time of signing this agreement, you shall pay us $____ as a nonrefundable advance against expenses. If the advance exceeds expenses incurred, the credit balance shall be used to reduce the fee payable or, if the fee has been fully paid, shall be reimbursed to you. Expenses shall in no event include any portion of our overhead.

9. Payment. You agree to pay us within ____ days of receipt of our billings for remuneration, expenses, or purchases of merchandise or construction. Overdue payments shall be subject to interest charges of ____ percent monthly. In the event that we are the winning party in a lawsuit brought pursuant to this agreement, you shall reimburse us for the costs of the lawsuit, including attorney's fees.

10. Term and Termination. This agreement shall have a term that expires on _____, 20__ The term shall automatically renew for additional _____ periods unless notice of termination is given either by us or you thirty (30) calendar days in advance of the renewal commencement. In addition, this agreement may be terminated at any time for cause by either party notifying the other party in writing of that party's breach of the Agreement and giving ten (10) business days for a cure, after which the notifying party may terminate if there has been no cure of the breach. Causes for termination shall include, but not be limited to, failure to perform any duty pursuant to this agreement in a timely manner and postponements of the Project for more than ____ business days in total. While reserving all other rights under this Agreement, in the event that the Project is terminated, we shall have the right to be paid by you through the date of termination for our work, for any purchases by us of merchandise and construction pursuant to purchase orders approved by you, and for our expenses.

11. Ownership of Design. We shall retain ownership of the design, including any drawings, renderings, sketches, samples, or other materials prepared by us during the course of the Project. Our ownership shall include any copyrights, trademarks, patents, or other proprietary rights existing in the design. You shall not use the design for additions to this Project or for any other project without obtaining our permission and paying appropriate compensation.

12. Consultants. If outside consultants, including but not limited to architects, structural engineers, mechanical engineers, acoustical engineers, and lighting designers, are needed for the Project, they shall be retained and paid for by you, and we shall cooperate fully with these consultants. Such consultants shall be responsible for code compliance in the various areas of their expertise.

13. Publicity. We shall have the right to document the Project in progress and when completed, by photography or other means, which we may use for portfolio, brochure, public display, and similar publicity purposes. Your name and the location of the Project may be used in connection with the documentation, unless specified to the contrary _____. If we choose to document the Project, we shall pay the costs of documentation. In addition, if you document the Project, we shall be given credit as the designer for the Project if your documentation is released to the public.

14. Relationship of Parties. We and you are both independent contractors. This agreement is not an employment agreement, nor does it constitute a joint venture or partnership between us and you. Nothing contained herein shall be construed to be inconsistent with this independent contractor relationship.

15. Assignment. Neither our nor your rights and duties may be assigned by either party without the written consent of the other party, except that we may assign payments due hereunder.

16. Arbitration. All disputes arising under this Agreement shall be submitted to binding arbitration before _____ in the following location _____ and settled in accordance with the rules of the American Arbitration Association. Judgment upon the arbitration award may be entered in any court having jurisdiction thereof. Disputes in which the amount at issue is less than $____ shall not be subject to this arbitration provision.

17. Miscellany. This agreement shall be binding on both us and you, as well as heirs, successors, assigns, and personal representatives. This agreement constitutes the entire understanding. Its terms can be modified only by an instrument in writing signed by both us and you. Notices shall be sent by certified mail or traceable overnight delivery to us or you at our present addresses, and notification of any change of address shall be given prior to that change of address taking effect. A waiver of a breach of any of the provisions of this agreement shall not be con-strued as a continuing waiver of other breaches of the same or other provisions hereof. This agreement shall be governed by the laws of the State of _____.

If this agreement meets with your approval, please sign beneath the words "Agreed to" to make this a binding agreement between us and you. Please sign both copies and return one copy for our files. We look forward to working with you.

AGREED TO

Sincerely yours,
XYZ Interior Design, Inc.

By: _____   By: _____
       Alice Client   Authorized Signatory, Title

Chapter 9: Public Relations

--- ✜ ---

When it comes to interior design, the ultimate form of recognition is bestowed upon a designer by the media, especially the publishing industry. What makes this type of thank-you so valuable and respected is that you cannot buy it; you have to earn it. When publications have legitimate editorial departments that operate independently from their publishing departments, they become arbiters of taste, and the designers they feature will be seen as desirable by the people who buy that publication. Once a designer's work is published, it receives a valuable seal of approval. An independent source is certifying that you are important and that what you do is worth sharing with their audience. This free, highly coveted exposure is called publicity.

The ironic part about publicity is that most designers do not get immediate business referrals from the coverage. While people may notice, they probably won't immediately pick up the phone and hire you for their own, similar projects. My hunch is that immediately following an appearance, the recipient may be perceived as "too hot," with pricing that reflects their level of fame. So, people tend to wait a bit before calling. Nonetheless, exposure makes you much more credible, so you should refer to it in all your marketing materials, including your Web site, promotional package, and portfolio. You can also bring it up casually in conversation: "Did you happen to see *House Beautiful* last month?" The fact that you have been published sends a very important message to potential clients; it says that you are exceptional at what you do, not because you say so but because other people say so. And depending upon the scope of the coverage and the publication—whether it is local, regional, or national—your ability to secure work outside of your area may hinge upon that recognition.

Immediate Needs

So, how do you get this elusive prize known as publicity? Media is a very "now" business: the right story at the right time gets attention. Editors can only focus on what they have in front of them, targeting specific deadlines. So, while your story may be interesting, it has to solve a need this week or this month to be given a second glance. This holds true for print (newspapers, journals, magazines), radio, television, and the Internet. One of the most important things you can do to increase odds of coverage is to know what an editor needs at that particular moment and present only pertinent work.

See if the publication you are targeting has an editorial calendar. (You can usually get this from the Web site or the ad sales representative.) The calendar may tell you that in March they are featuring wicker furniture. Have you just finished a wonderful conservatory featuring exotic wicker? You might want to contact an editor in December and let them know that you have just designed a room that might be perfect for the wicker feature. Keep in mind that different publications have different lead times: the editor will tell you if you are too late or too early. If you are too late, then present your project again (or to another editor) later on—perhaps for the conservatory issue in June!

Your job is to figure out who is interested in what—and when. A story about a rescued cat is relevant to your neighborhood weekly, not *USA Today*—unless, of course, there is something outstanding to report, such as the cat was heard meowing at the bottom of an elevator shaft at the New York Stock Exchange Building and necessitated a daring rescue by a repairman. Oh, and someone was around to take pictures. In that case, the story might get written up in the *Wall Street Journal.*

The Right Match

If you want coverage for your beautiful, recently completed interior design project, you need to match it with an appropriate media outlet. First, consider the type of aesthetic it embodies: a contemporary home does not belong in *Traditional Home* magazine. Consider, also, the caliber of the design and furnishings. Be realistic to avoid disappointment. Is your project really worthy of *Architectural Digest* or would it be better suited to a local publication? The local publication might actually get your work in front of your likeliest clients.

If you are uncertain about whom to approach with your project or story, go to a bookstore or library and scan a few publications to see which ones cover the type of work you have. Additionally, try to identify a writer whose writing style or aesthetic appeals to you, and address your submission to them. I would choose the most unobtrusive way to make contact, allowing the writer time to respond, and this would be through e-mail, if you can find or figure out the address. (Usually, companies have the same e-mail protocol, so if the editor is *Jennifer.Green@finemag.com*, you can be fairly sure that their staff writer, Peter Woolsy, can be reached at *Peter.Woolsy@finemag.com*.) This situation is, by the way, one of the few instances in which I favor an e-mail-contact first. Alternatively, you can write the appropriate editor a letter outlining your interests and including relevant materials to best acquaint them with what you do and why it might be of interest. (I will describe these materials later in this chapter.)

Following this initial contact, I would wait a week or two, then follow up with a phone call if you have not received a response. Remember to preface the call by asking for permission to take their time. If time is granted, immediately explain that you are following up on your previously sent communication and simply want confirmation that it was received. If not, assure the editor that you will promptly resend and say you will follow up again in a few days. Should they be too busy to speak at that moment, ask for the best time to try them back, making note of what they say. Make sure you follow their instructions, as editors often have very specific times they prefer to be contacted. Call back at their specified time, and again explain your purpose for the call. If you get voicemail, I would not leave a message; I recommend instead trying again at a different time of day a few days later. After your third attempt, leave a message, then call again in a week.

Hearing Back

My experience with submitting content to editors suggests that if they are interested in your materials, you will hear back from them in short order. However, if the editors are not interested, they will generally not respond at all. This can be maddening when you consider that it only takes a minute to write, "Thank you for your note, but we have already decided which rooms we will use for our wicker feature." Still, that's the way of the world, and it's only rarely that you will receive a courtesy "no, thank you" or a referral to a more appropriate editor on staff. If you do get an e-mail rejection, and the editor is not specific about why, you can always ask for feedback, keeping in mind that the editor has a busy schedule or may not want to bother, and you may not hear anything at all.

In attempting to manage your own publicity, never be discouraged by a rejection or lack of response from one or several editors. They do not speak for the entire media industry—just for themselves and their particular needs. If my firm is unsuccessful pitching projects in the U.S., we look to other countries. A "thank you" from a legitimate publication anywhere in the world is still a "thank you," and seeing your rooms in an Italian magazine can make you feel like an international player.

Different Markets, Different Needs

Each market has different needs; the focus changes according to the audience. For example, the local station is interested in the room you designed for a local hospice house project, whereas its national affiliate is interested in an emerging trend surrounding hospice house design that will likely influence other organizations. You need to massage the story you are pitching to the specific publication. Unfortunately, blanket approaches are generally ineffective, with the exception of editorial targeted for media Web sites that can be accessed through distribution services (we use PR Newswire for our clients). There are so many Web sites out there that unless the story is total rubbish, you are going to get picked up somewhere, although a hit from a prospect in Des Moines might not matter if your practice is based in LA. At any rate, generally you must target your editors and tailor your pitch so that they see that the story is relevant to their audience.

A few years ago, my company was representing a designer from Silver Spring, Maryland, who markets herself as the family designer—

someone who knows how to deal with kids, pets, and messy husbands. She is a lot of fun, with enough energy to fuel a jet, so she was a pleasure to work with and package for multiple opportunities. Initially, given that she is a talented designer, we went to lifestyle publications that would be interested in the basic residential coverage. Then, we decided to approach parenting publications, highlighting the special fabrics and paint she uses to resist everyday spills and drills from families with children. Next, we pitched pet publications, since she designs "pet friendly" homes with the requisite flooring and fabric to survive a pet's wear and tear. And finally, the most out-of-the-box pitch we created for this designer was the husband-as-slob angle. We were able to go to newspapers, magazines, radio stations, and television media with these various pitches. This designer's publicity goal was her own television show. She didn't get that, but our efforts ultimately resulted in two television interviews for her. In addition, she received press coverage from a variety of other favorable outlets, and the kids and pet pitches got the most play of all.

Speaking of play, Laura is a client from Scottsdale, Arizona. While she is a terrific designer, there are many talented professionals in the Scottsdale area. What could we do to promote her? We decided that her unique angle was . . . baseball: one of America's favorite pastimes. She had completed projects for a number of professional ball players: Scottsdale is home to the sport's spring training hub. Crafting a story around baseball appeals to sports publications as well as to interior and design magazines, and we placed several stories in sports magazines. Furthermore, we were able to leverage this designer's baseball experience by approaching different sports agents and getting them to pitch her services to players on the teams they manage.

The PR Firm

Sometimes people ask me if they should hire a public relations (PR) firm. I say the decision depends on time and money. You can learn the necessary ways to promote yourself to the media by reading to the end of this chapter. But do you actually want to commit to promoting yourself? Do you have the time it takes to network and build and maintain rapport with media? If not, consider hiring an experienced PR firm. Buyer beware: there are many people who hang out a shingle, promising results with media relations, and sadly, don't deliver. An easy way to gauge a service is by what the firm charges. A legitimate firm will ask for a retainer fee that averages $3,000 per month for its services. I know this is a lot of money for a small business to invest, particularly when a year is the recommended commitment to achieve certain objectives, but there is no shortcut to securing desirable publicity—despite the occasional success story that seems to have developed overnight.

When you sign up for a year of PR services, you are paying for an experienced professional to package and prepare you for the media. You are paying for their ability to target the right media at the right time. Additionally, you are paying for their long-established relationships with the media, which gives them entrée to editors you might never access. This does not guarantee that the relationship will result in coverage, since good editorial is based on the merit of the content, but having access to who your PR guy knows certainly can't hurt. And last, you are paying for the publicist to be at the right places at the right times on your behalf. So much of media relations is based on being out in the field, networking, being aware, and being informed. This takes time and therefore money, most of which is not directly billed to you but amortized over many clients within the firm's monthly retainers. Boutique PR firms often operate out of one location within a specific region. However, if you are seeking national coverage, you really should consider a firm with multiple offices, ideally located on both coasts, since this is where editors tend to congregate—the exception being the Meredith Corporation in Des Moines, publishers of *Better Homes & Gardens* and *Traditional Home* and one of my favorite companies. Its staff are friendly, return calls, and don't take themselves too seriously.

PR BILLING

In addition to a monthly retainer fee, you will likely be invoiced for expenses associated with your account, including the cost of press materials, couriers, travel, and entertainment. Some firms charge lower retainers, making up for it in expenses billed at a mark-up of 10 to 20 percent. The best way to determine which type of billing works best for you is to ask what the estimated expenses will be on top of the monthly retainer and factor that number into the entire period to which you are willing to commit. Be sure to ask how long they expect it will take to get results. The PR industry is not an exact science, and publicists are only as good as the material they have to work with. In other words, if the project is not representative of good design, it is not going to get published in any publication of note, regardless of added fluff from a well-crafted pitch. Or, if the story is not newsworthy (such as your new hires or a new office opening), the pitch will be relegated to a quick mention, if it is used at all. Perhaps the most important question you can ask a PR representative is if they think you have what it takes to warrant an all-out investment in media relations. Be honest about your dreams, goals, and expectations so they can, in turn, be honest about what they are able to deliver. It's a reasonable question; be prepared for an honest answer. (Or for a dishonest answer, if they really want your business.) Perhaps the best idea is to work with a PR firm that has done well for someone at about your level of experience, so ask around.

THE MEDIA MACHINE

During the early formation of my company's media relations or PR division, I worked with a designer who boasts very elegant work for equally elegant and very wealthy clients. We pitched him to various publications, and to our disbelief, received one "no thank you" after another. Something was always amiss: either the rooms were not quite right, or we did not portray them fully finished, or the aesthetic was unclear, or the photography was too bland. We kept trying, but we were unable to get any significant coverage for him in the traditional sense. However, we did create a number of speaking opportunities for him and used these appearances to arrange as many introductions to editors as possible. Was this a successful campaign? In the short term, probably not. Did we exhaust all efforts to serve our client? Yes, we did. Sometimes, coverage just does not happen. However, we've probably paved the way for future coverage, and the client is content for the time being.

Sometimes, however, the timing is just right and the media machine does what it is supposed to do. Lanie is an active client who sprung a project on us at short notice: she wanted to launch her furniture collection in High Point, North Carolina during one of the regularly scheduled bi-annual markets. With scarcely more than two weeks to package, pitch, and launch her collection, we managed to get our client in the *Wall Street Journal Weekend Journal,* on local television, and in numerous trade publications that promoted her story and furniture collection. The campaign was decisively executed and was a resounding success. This was an example of ideal sync in timing and media interest: the hook was the bi-annual show (it's good to have an event to make the story timely), the client was promotable, and her furniture was truly outstanding.

Results such as hers are the culmination of hard work, good timing, and a little bit of luck. This is possible to achieve on an individual basis if you take the time to prepare your materials and follow up on all submissions in a methodical manner. For your PR campaign you will need a proper media kit, a well-crafted press release, great photography, and the ability to research those sources from which you want coverage. Let's take a look at each of these items so that you can give this a shot.

Media Kit

Your media kit is an integral tool for your business; it is something that evolves as your business does. It is usually contained in a colored cover with pockets for your info and a place for your business card. A media kit will typically include your biography, testimonials, details about your firm, staff biographies, notable projects, samples of your work, and reprints of press you have received.

The biography (which should not be longer than a page) will illustrate your background in a compelling manner, highlighting qualities for which you want to be known and what kind of clients you want to attract—those with money, people who like to have fun, art collectors, people who are very hands-on, or those who don't want to lift a finger for their projects. If you are just building your business, your answer may well be, "I need clients! I want to design for all of them!" In that case, make sure nothing in your bio discourages people in any category from hiring you. If you are lucky enough to pick and choose your clients, and you prefer to work with collectors, you should highlight your expertise in the art world and with other collectors.

Here especially, testimonials from satisfied clients will serve you well. Collector A will be impressed that collector B is singing your praises. As with all testimonials, you need to list the first and last name of the individual as well as the city and state in which he or she resides in order for the testimonial to be considered credible. That way, if someone wants to call the source, they can.

Depending upon the size of your firm, you may have a separate firm biography highlighting the accomplishments of the business as a whole. This is particularly germane if you are not the original owner, are one of several principals, or are specifically trying to highlight the firm and not you individually. The bios of other staff members should be short, a paragraph at most. Consider putting several on the same page. Headshots are good to include in all instances.

Your project tear sheets should include two to five images of work that you have done, grouping different aesthetics and specialties together on one page. If you have a solid body of work in a traditional style, you can show these examples separately from your work on modern houses. Similarly, you should group residential projects together, separate from commercial projects. You do not need descriptions of the projects, just your firm's contact information on each page.

Past media coverage can include projects that have been published, articles you have written, articles written about you, or instances in which your name has been mentioned, like a list of the top ten designers in your area. For published work, I recommend a color copy of the front cover of the publication and copies of the editorial pages. If you have been published more than a handful of times, just include the best, most recent examples, and then have a one-sheet, featuring covers of publications, reduced to fit on a single page; readers will be impressed.

Your media kit can be sent to anybody who has an interest in your work, including media, potential clients, and potential referral sources. When sending a media kit to potential clients, I recommend adding a copy of your standard letter of agreement so they know you will require one with your services. With respect to media sources, you can approach magazines, newspapers, radio station, television stations, and more recently, bloggers. Depending upon your desired area of coverage, you can go after local (your city or those immediately surrounding), regional (within a few hundred miles or possibly your state), national, and international media outlets. Is the list of prospects potentially large? Absolutely! And knowing which ones to go after takes time, patience, and yes, experience. A PR professional will know who is most likely to respond to your queries.

THE PRESS RELEASE

The next item to develop is the press release. There are zillions of samples on the Internet, so I'm not going to take too much time explaining. Rather, I encourage you to do some research for examples and formats to reference. In composing a press release, you need to answer the who, what, when, where, and why questions as quickly as you can, crafting your most gripping statement, known as "the hook," in the first sentence of your release. It is important to note that most things, such as moving offices or adding staff, are not newsworthy per se, except in very limited instances. You might get a new staff announcement picked up in a trade journal, but unless it's read by potential clients, this type of coverage is generally not worth the effort required. If you sign on to do the model homes for a new residential community, such news could be of interest to your local real estate editor and possibly the lifestyles editor as well. There are certain hot-buttons for media that you can monitor in the media outlets that you follow. Sustainability, universal design, aging-in-place, and historic preservation are likely to interest the media for some time to come.

The most important aspect of creating a press release is to get your point or the hook across as quickly as you can. Here's one example of the hook in a press release: "*Specialty Interiors*, a residential design firm in Pensacola, has just helped an elderly couple keep their home and age gracefully in an environment they trust." If the majority of an editor's readership is over fifty years old, chances are this one sentence in your press release will inspire the editor to read further. Following the hook, you should briefly answer the key questions the message might inspire (i.e., where was the home? what changes were made? how much did it cost?), making sure the paragraph can be printed in its entirety, if desired. And it is often desired. Editors are busy, and you'll be surprised to find how many will just print your release verbatim—sometimes under someone else's byline.

Additional information to include in your release could be a list of the builders and manufacturers who teamed up for the project. This gives them much-deserved credit and creates more of a business angle to the story. The participants will appreciate the mention, and including additional sources makes your work look more important. Following the body of the press release, add a standard paragraph, commonly called the boilerplate, giving details about you and your firm for the editor to incorporate into the write-up. The boilerplate is something that should always be at the end of the release.

ADVERTISING

I want to close this chapter by taking a look at the sibling of public relations: advertising. Advertising builds brands, but advertising programs are expensive to execute effectively because most require consistency (insertions for a span of one year or more) and breadth (multiple publications that target the same audience). It is almost impossible to determine whether or not your target audience is going to be reading the particular issue in which your ad is placed, so in order to increase odds for visibility to your audience, you will need to run multiple ads in consistent publications over a generous amount of time. After all, your goal is for potential clients to remember your name when the time comes to pick up the phone and find a designer.

Depending upon the publication, you may spend a few hundred to several thousand dollars per ad.

Ad rates are determined by a publication's circulation, so the more eyes that see it, the more money you can expect to pay. While discounts are provided for multiple insertions, your per-insertion rate is not going to discount more than approximately 20 percent. A quality regional magazine may quote an ad rate of $2,000–$3,000 per full-page placement, per issue, while at the same time, a prestigious national publication such as *Architectural Digest* can run upwards of $80,000 per full-page placement, per issue. Stepping down from the full-page ad, a smaller placement of a quarter-page ad in a local publication might be as low as $50, but is placed towards the back of a circular, which limits your responses. On the other hand, the outer back cover is a great place for an ad and usually commands a very high premium. The old saying rings true when it comes to advertising: you get what you pay for.

Take a close look at your goals for advertising, and realistically examine your options and budget. Study media kits of your preferred publications and call current advertisers listed to inquire about their experience with advertising and their return on investment. The next step after performing the necessary legwork is to contact your regional sales representative for rates and a customized program to meet your needs. Remember, the purpose of an ad sales representative is to sell you space in their publication, and most will have a good argument about why you should sign on with them as opposed to the competition. I can always spot the sales reps at an industry party because they are the ones who are rather attractive, extraordinarily friendly, and happy to talk to you, me, him, her—and that guy over there across the room. Understandably, the editors (in great demand because they can confer fame on a designer with one glowing story at no cost to the designer) keep to themselves.

Now, before my friends in publishing close this book and cut me dead, let me proclaim that some of the best relationships I have are with people in sales who either work directly for the publisher—or who *are* the publishers. In addition to placing your ad favorably, publishers can promote you at events and give you opportunities that do not come from editors. They can co-sponsor events, assist you in mailing to their databases, and provide gift bag items, copies of their publication, and creative co-branding opportunities. You see, they have the money. So, if you are considering advertising, see what else comes with the package. They call these benefits "perks" or "value added" elements. Sometimes it's the extras that make an ad program worthwhile.

Chapter 10: RIDING THE TRENDS

---------------------------- ❖ ----------------------------

As I write this book, the U.S. and the global economy are experiencing the symptoms of a recession. Although it hasn't hit quite yet, many businesses are exhibiting signs of trouble, from lower sales volume to increased pressure on pricing. Today, it's more important than ever to stay abreast of changes in public sentiment and needs.

The single largest factor in the current economic slow-down is attributed to the mortgage crisis and the ensuing softening of the real estate market. A combination of easy credit standards and a surplus in real property supply exposed the questionable lending practices of the finance industry as a whole. Almost all financial institutions have suffered staggering losses, forcing some of the most reputable firms into bankruptcy or failure. In a nutshell, the institutions were lending more money than consumers could ultimately pay back, and in many instances, more than the properties were worth, especially when the market shifted and prices declined. Some lenders would lend up to 100 percent of the purchase price and more, so just about anyone could own a piece of the American dream. While it definitely provides access to home ownership, this sort of lending is certainly not prudent, as we now have learned. Many people with "no income verification" mortgages cannot meet their payments and are losing their houses.

You might be thinking that these people do not represent the typical interior design client, and you are absolutely correct. So, you may be wondering why this is relevant.

THE CREDIT CRUNCH

When the credit market started to retreat, raising lending standards and restricting loans, the real estate market experienced a slow-down in sales, and people found it harder to get mortgages. This credit crunch helped engender falling real estate values, the foundation for the former paper wealth of U.S. consumers. Furthermore, falling equity was joined with consumer uncertainty for a bumpy ride down the path of reduced spending. In addition, bankers, brokers, real estate attorneys, finance attorneys—anybody who touched the mortgage industries or the institutions affected by the crisis, people who *do* meet the profile of the interior design client, either lost their bonuses, lost their jobs, or stopped spending for fear of losing their jobs. Not a pretty picture for the residential designer.

You might be thinking that there are many very wealthy people in the world who still have money to spend, and you are absolutely correct. However, these same people, in many instances, are deciding to be socially conscious and curb their more obvious spending habits out of solidarity for those less fortunate. While this behavior is admirable, it just keeps pushing down on the economy, driving it further toward the dreaded "R" word.

Now, this same group is fueling the sales and growth of the luxury brands that sell leather handbags, scarves, jewelry, and anything else that is opulent or that can be construed as an investment-grade must-have (like an expensive watch that should keep its value). Think about it: your prospects can spend $3,000 on something special and feel good while holding off on that $300,000 renovation they had been planning. After all, it was only for their third home, which they use infrequently.

Having said all this, I know that there are the very wealthy or those that don't care what other people think who are still proceeding with projects—and bless them for that. However, we need to realize that behaviors and spending habits do change for one reason or another, and it is imperative that you pay attention and package your services and products accordingly. In this case, I cannot stress enough that you need to focus on the one item that is valuable regardless of the economy: your individual talent. Nobody else in the world designs just the way you do or behaves (for better or worse) just the way you do, so what you have to sell is truly unique.

Your Passion and Your Gift

The interior design business is about passion; it's about the visceral feeling that makes a person intuitively know what works or doesn't work in design and the thrill that accompanies implementing solutions that bring other people joy. While this may sound a bit heady, it is entirely true. Why else wake up in the morning and face a blank room or house that requires numerous ideas and combinations of solutions in order to solve a physical or aesthetic problem? This is an artistic endeavor that combines a lot of knowledge, a bit of engineering, and a great deal of creativity. Most people simply don't have that combination of talents. Interior design ability is a gift that needs to be treated as such and not minimized as something that anyone can do—because they can't. The challenge is packaging this gift effectively when perceptions change and the market is influenced by factors beyond your control. The twelve-step people have the right idea about accepting the things you cannot change (the economy), changing the things you can (your approach), and having the wisdom to know the difference.

DESIGN SERVICES BY RETAIL STORES

Let's look at a big factor affecting the industry: the influx of retail stores that provide design services for free to consumers (it's almost like a gift with a purchase). It is important to recognize that this is not the first time retail stores have provided design departments for their consumers. In fact, much of the industry as we know it originated from fancy stores like B. Altman, which sold furniture and had teams of designers who catered to its customers. This did not stop independent interior designers from flourishing because they were able to capitalize on two factors: relationships and resources.

As with many service industries, the design business depends on referral or word of mouth; in other words, it depends on people being happy with their designers and being vocal about it. People who can afford a design professional really care what their friends think and will often ask for referrals for service providers in all categories, including designers. This is not to say that people may not be enticed into a store and then start working with a designer there, but they will continue to work with the designer because they formed a relationship with him or her. Without that relationship, there would not be a successful outcome to the project. So, unless every design prospect in the world walks into a retail store and gets his or her needs met, there will always be those who venture into the realm of independent designers, have a positive experience, and influence their friends to use that same designer.

There is also one more factor to consider: the word "free." Nothing is free in this world, and services provided by stores are not free either. The cost of design services is bundled with the cost of the product, so the consumer pays an inflated price on the product. It is very important to point this out to clients, so that you minimize the effect of the false advertising. More truthful advertising would say that the interior design services are not charged separately from the cost of the merchandise. You can't change the way they market their services, but you can change the way you market yours.

The majority of designers once worked on a cost-plus basis only, charging, as their design fee, a commission on the product sold. As we have seen, some designers still use this model. The consumer receives a proposal for product, and the price quoted is all-inclusive of product and services. However, this pricing method poses a challenge in that it is possible for a designer to design, shop, and present countless options while the client chooses to purchase very little or even nothing, leaving the designer without adequate (and sometimes without any) compensation. The solution to this problem is to obtain an up-front, non-refundable retainer to be applied against future commissions, if any, in exchange for the design time invested. I realize that a prospect may protest that they can go to XYZ store and get design services without paying a deposit and then only be obligated for what they actually buy. This is a reasonable argument to which you can reply, "The trade-off is that an independent designer can purchase from an unlimited number of resources and, in many cases, find better values than an in-store designer can. So, I save you money while providing a greater assortment of merchandise and aesthetics and ultimately, the best possible design solutions." Retail store designers cannot make this claim.

CLIENTS' NEEDS FIRST!

In response to the situation created by retail store policies, it is important to remember that you are providing clients with a professional service and to disclose the cost of that service in advance. You are not beholden to one source, and since you do not work solely on commission, you, unlike store personnel, are not motivated by the sale of merchandise in order to be compensated. You have the clients' needs firmly in mind and make decisions that will be most beneficial to the client in the short-term and long-term (better quality products can last longer and be cheaper when amortized over the years). Remember; sell the design solutions and the process of design, not the products. Product is a commodity; your ideas are not.

It is good to be very specific so that your prospects understand the advantages of working with you. If your area has a high-end furniture store that offers design services (say, Maurice Villency), take off a couple of hours and visit it, pretending that you are a client. Ask for some standard items—a cream-colored sofa, a glass coffee table, a display cabinet. Note what they suggest and how many items they offer for each, noting the prices. (You should refresh these examples from one year to the next.) Now, go out on your own and find better and less expensive examples of these, being sure to capture images either online or by photographing the products. Now you have evidence to back your assertion that even with your fee, your clients spend less on you than they would at the store—and get more choice, to boot.

TELEVISION AND FALSE EXPECTATIONS

Retailers are not alone in their quest to capture market share; they have an accomplice. The culprit is none other than television shows that espouse the wonders of design, especially with minimal budgets on impossibly short schedules. Over the last several years, there has been an influx of design-related television shows, many under the HGTV production umbrella. These have certainly raised design awareness for the general public. This awareness is neither a clear-cut blessing nor a curse, but it needs further investigation. First, this isn't reality TV; it's *un*reality TV that plants unrealistic expectations in the minds of consumers. These shows are created to capture ratings and promote the products of the advertisers featured in each segment.

Design just happens to be the vehicle for this promotional effort and has ultimately increased the public's awareness of design. I have not said the "value" of design, because that is quashed by skimpy budgets and schedules. What viewers don't see are the teams of people who work behind the scenes to make things happen, sourcing the product well in advance, and then building and assembling rooms in an eye-blink, to the amazement of the audience. The result is that people actually believe you can have a fabulous room for $1,000 in only one day. This is where the problem begins.

I have spoken with many designers who have participated in *Designer's Challenge* and similar shows, and their response is always, "Never again!" True, they may get a videotape of the episode. They may even get an occasional phone call from a viewer, but it is usually to find out where the designer purchased a specific pillow or from someone who thinks that they, too, can get local design professionals to compete for their $20,000 project, furnishing complete storyboards in the process. Now, if you need something for your portfolio, you might give "reality" TV a shot, just to obtain the footage. However, if you are a seasoned professional with a firm client base, then I would not participate in this caliber of programming, which creates false expectations and a shocked silence for potential customers when they learn about the *real* dollars and time needed to complete a project. The next time people tell you about instant, budget TV makeovers, just laugh and say, "Those shows aren't reality—they're entertainment!"

SMALL PACKAGES

The naïve prospect who calls a designer after watching a TV design show needs to be qualified as to whether or not she has the financial wherewithal to hire a real design professional. Then, the prospect needs to be educated about the process of design. If there's gold in those hills, you should mine it. Now, in order to take advantage of this newly enlightened public, I would encourage designers to have a special package deal that can be offered to callers. While $1,000 will not buy much of anything, what could you do with $5,000 at IKEA? Could you take $1,500 for your time that day and then invest the other $3,500 in enough cool products to make a client happy? Much of what you do is artistic and has to do with accessories and "layering" that most people cannot even imagine, although they appreciate when they see it. I'm sure that most designers could create ambiance with candles and floral arrangements, let alone with the vast amount of merchandise you can buy for $3,500 in a store like IKEA.

This is not, of course, an endorsement of discount stores. It is rather a strong recommendation that each designer be willing to work on small projects that have quick solutions and immediate timeframes. You, the designer, can (and should) shop anywhere and always be of service to clients, as long as your time is valued. This helps you generate some cash while waiting for that juicy full-service project for which you have been praying. Remember that through marriage, inheritance, or personal success, today's IKEA customer can turn into tomorrow's design center customer who remembers how great is was to work with you. At that point, the client will be a valuable source of referrals. A satisfied customer at any level is a positive reinforcement of your professionalism and talent as a designer. We don't have to work just for the rich and can in fact bring good design to the masses. It just requires rethinking the way projects are structured and providing service in affordable increments. You are not discounting your service; you are merely selling less of it to that particular client.

DIY

There is another facet of this that we need to explore: the dreaded do-it-yourself (DIY) market. Most designers have shunned this segment because of its propensity to encourage the general public to take ideas and implement them on their own, without the trusted help of a design professional. These people, many of whom could well afford a designer, just choose to do the design and implementation on their own.

Everything boils down to offering the right service or product at the right price in order to make a sale. Therefore, it behooves designers to determine which of their services they can sell to the DIY crowd. The solution is pretty tough, but not impossible, and one of my clients has figured out a way to tap this market.

Richard's customers provide him with photos and measurements and he, in turn, provides custom design solutions that they fulfill from retail sources—on their own. The custom design is provided from accessible sources like Pottery Barn, Rugs Direct, Lamps Plus, and any retail source with an on-line store. The customers are provided with a list of product, a floor plan, and directions for placement, and then they just implement the plan when they are ready to, on their own schedule and when their budgets permit. In fact, they can scale the products according to quality, using products provided as a guideline only or selecting more or less expensive merchandise if they desire. Here is the surprising part: each room costs only $299 for the custom design. Yes, that's right, $299 to have an interior designer plan a room.

Before you close your business down and start looking at educational courses in another field (physician's assistant? paralegal? sky-diver?), please bear in mind that the person who elects to hire this cut-rate design service is probably not the same person that could afford to or would choose to hire a full-service design professional in the first place. Richard is cleverly addressing a market that has previously been underserved. My challenge to each of you is to figure out a market segment to serve, no matter how small, then create a custom offering exclusively for them (because everyone likes the idea of exclusivity) and invest in the promotional machinery needed to make the concept a success.

There is a wonderful book by Harold Evans, *They Made America: From the Steam Engine to the Search Engine: Two Centuries of Innovators*, which details the fascinating triumphs of America's inventors. The premise of the book is that it is not sufficient to have a good idea: it is necessary to bring that idea to the marketplace, and in many cases, create the marketplace in order for the idea to become commercially successful.

SPECIALIZATION

This takes us to the last item: specialization. I have met hundreds of designers over the years who have asked me to assess their business cards, apart from the design. These queries usually follow a presentation that I have made on marketing in which I discuss the image that is created by marketing materials. What I inevitably comment on is the multiple service listings that they have on their cards including furniture, design, shopping service, graphic design, contracting, architecture, staging, real estate sales, notary public—and occasionally *trompe l'oeil* and needlepoint! Just because you can do something doesn't mean you should promote it at the same time you promote your core services. Moreover, I suggest that you are better off being more specific about what you do so that you can be among the few, not the many, that do what you do.

During speaking presentations, I frequently ask for a show of hands to see how many people specialize or have training in currently growing areas of design, including sustainability, aging-in-place, hospitality, feng shui, and institutional design. Inevitably, there will only be a few hands that are raised for any one specialty, and I encourage people to look around and see how much of their perceived competition has just dropped out. If there are 100 designers in an audience and only five raise their hands acknowledging expertise in aging-in-place, it stands to reason that their chances of getting the project are better than those of the other ninety-five when called on by an aging-in-place client. Furthermore, when someone is doing a search for a specialist in any field, the odds of getting consideration in a pool of five is significantly greater than when in the pool of 100.

It is important to remember that just because you are specializing (as evidenced by your marketing materials), it does not mean you must say no to other types of projects. It does mean, however, that your emphasis is on your specialization, and that you focus your attention on gaining that type of business. I liken this to hunting. If you want a specific animal, you use a rifle and target your prey. If you don't care what you get or are shooting a moving target (say, a bird), you use a shotgun so that the blast covers a larger area. Of course, you may hit something that you hadn't intended on hitting. So in marketing, you must be targeted and specific in order to get the results you seek. As I've mentioned earlier, you need to have your name in front of your target market six to eight times during a calendar year, and choosing a specialty allows you to focus on a specific group, for example, the aging-in-place folks. You know that they are going to be sixty-plus years old and will probably have lived in their homes for more than ten years. That narrows your target so it is easier to hit. If you were to just choose anyone who needs residential design services, then that would significantly increase your target area and require more money to adequately solicit prospects.

A last note on the subject of specialization: consider how many people introduce themselves as "high-end residential interior designers." While I don't have the exact figures, I can tell you from the 100-plus speaking presentations I have done in markets all over the United States that better than 50 percent of my audiences identify with this description. The first question I usually ask at this point is, "What is 'high-end'?" High-end to one person may mean a project valued at $30,000, while to another a it might be a project valued at $250,000. So, think of the confusion or misrepresentation that can ensue from the introduction that most designers make. My hope is that you will take the time to continue your education and research in the field of design and hone your skills in an area of interest that allows you to legitimately claim and promote yourself as a specialist. Then, see how your business improves.

Chapter 11: GOING GREEN

❖

Today, environmental awareness affects everything we do. Once the province of the educated elite, going green has spread to the mainstream. IBM makes "end of life" plans for its computers; restaurants offer organic veggies and fish from sustainable stock; e-mail comes with reminders such as, "Do not print unless absolutely necessary." Even Wal-Mart is getting into the act with the sale of curly energy-saving light bulbs and the local sourcing of many products. Guarding our precious and limited natural resources—air, water, oil—is no longer controversial; it's a common goal. Al Gore's film, *An Inconvenient Truth*, brought knowledge of global warming to the general public. Although a few people question some of his numbers, I doubt anyone disagrees with his message that we must all become stewards of our environment so that future generations can live on a benign and beautiful planet Earth.

While environmental awareness affects everything, certain businesses, such as the building and design industry, now find themselves at the forefront of environmental change. This is natural: our buildings use a full 40 percent of the energy consumed in the United States. Just by making our new and old houses more energy-efficient, we can save billions of gallons of oil a year.

GREEN OPPORTUNITY

The green movement presents a significant growth opportunity for builders and designers alike. Many clients are quite happy with their layout and décor but are motivated to remodel by their conscience and their wallet. It's important to realize that some environmental upgrades pay for themselves in a year or two, after which they reduce expenses year after year.

Having a pure heart is one thing, but cutting expenses is the true motivator for change. Now that the price of gas has doubled in the past few years, consumers are finally changing their transportation behavior by implementing carpools, taking public transit, and even riding bikes to work. Suddenly, they are buying smaller cars and listening to what the environmentalists have been saying for decades. Some green activists welcome high gas prices in the U.S. because they prompt people to finally strategize about using less oil. Indeed, this may be the ideal moment to incorporate environmental awareness into your practice and to suggest sustainable processes and products to your clients.

ASID AND REGREEN

When it comes to the matter of sustainability, the American Society of Interior Designers (ASID) certainly thinks that having a succinct policy for use in practice (design) and promotion (marketing and advocacy) is a must. ASID is the professional association for interior designers, and it holds that "interior designers should endeavor to, whenever feasible, practice sustainable design. Interior designers should meet present-day needs without compromising the ability to meet the needs of future generations." If you visit its Web site, *www.asid.org*, you will see a wealth of educational and informational offerings to its members. You will also find a link to ReGreen, the result of a collaboration between ASID and the United States Green Building Council (USGBC). ReGreen believes that interior designers should play an active role in the environmental movement, advocating with their clients and employers for the development of buildings, spaces, and products that are environmentally friendly, produced in a socially just manner, and safe for all living things. ReGreen urges designers to bring up ecological issues and serve as educators to their clients. Some of ReGreen's principles include:

- **Protection of the Biosphere.** Interior designers should eliminate the use of any product or process that is known to pollute air, water, or earth.

- **Sustainable Use of Natural Resources.** Interior designers should make use of renewable natural resources, including the protection of vegetation, wildlife habitats, open spaces, and wilderness.

- **Waste Reduction.** Interior designers should minimize waste through the reduction, reuse, or recycling of products and encourage the development and use of reclaimed, salvaged, and recycled products.

- **Wise Use of Energy.** Interior designers should reduce energy use, adopt energy conserving strategies, and choose renewable energy sources.

- **Reduction of Risk.** Interior designers should eliminate the environmental risk to the health of the end users of their designs.

GREEN FOR HUMAN HEALTH

For one of my California clients, the health aspect of going green is the most significant. "It's important to think of the green movement in terms of human health as well as the environment. While it's sometimes difficult to get a client to pay 30 percent more for eco-friendly insulation they won't see once a structure is finished, it's easy to get someone to spend 100 percent more on vitamins that might give them more energy. I show my clients how better insulation will be better for their homes and for their health. Focusing on the effects of health in the green movement has made my practice grow and allowed me to follow my ideals about using earth-friendly methods and materials. This approach seems to hit home with my clientele."

Another of my clients, Lori Dennis in southern California, won *Home* magazine's coveted Green Designer of the Year Award after her firm designed a house for a young man who'd survived cancer. "Our client is a twenty-eight-year-old man who had testicular cancer throughout his childhood. He was fortunate to beat the disease and now focuses on living an organic, healthy lifestyle. With the purchase of his first property two years ago, he wasn't only interested in hiring a designer who had great taste, but one who could accommodate his healthy lifestyle and organic-based concerns. Because our firm specializes in all aspects of green design, we had an advantage over the other firms he interviewed. We could deliver everything he wanted and needed— and more."

Lori Dennis is doing well by doing good. She seized upon the opportunity that going green provides. By 2030, a full forty-million "green collar" jobs will be created, according to a recent AP story. These jobs will be in the renewable energy and energy-efficient industries. Colleges and universities are introducing specialized degree programs in eco-commerce, environmental accounting, green and social marketing, and ecological economics to prepare for the demand. The article notes that "there is also a growing demand for architects and engineers with Leadership in Energy and Environmental Design (LEED) certification from the U.S. Green Building Council."

LEED CERTIFICATION

LEED uses a green building rating system for environmentally sustainable construction developed by the USGBC. For new construction and major renovations for commercial buildings there are sixty-nine possible points, and buildings can qualify for four levels of certification:

- Certified: 26-32 points

- Silver: 33-38 points

- Gold: 39-51 points

- Platinum: 52-69 points

LEED certification is mandatory for some public buildings and a source of pride and prestige for owners of some private houses. You can be sure that if their home is LEED certified, the client will look for a green designer—one whose products are either recycled or locally sourced, and one who will reduce the carbon footprint of the house. A carbon footprint is not some charred foot shape in the sand; it is a measure of the impact our activities have on the environment as a whole and on climate change in particular. Your carbon footprint is directly related to the amount of greenhouse gases you produce by burning fossil fuels for electricity, heating, and transportation. Considering the global warming crisis, does anybody really need a 10,000-square-foot home with three cars in the driveway?

Given the obvious advantages of going green (to you, to your clients, and to the planet), why aren't all projects green? Two words: cost and selection.

THE COST OF GOING GREEN

The number one problem consumers face when it comes to using green products and materials instead of traditional, non-green options is that green versions cost approximately 10 to 15 percent more than their conventional counterparts. Depending on the scope of a project, consumers using green building materials run the risk of adding a considerable premium to an otherwise moderately-priced project. Design professionals need to educate clients on the long-term viability of the added costs by showing that any other decision might be detrimental to their health and increase likelihood of replacing products and materials, thus ultimately necessitating a bigger outlay. For instance, buying a traditional hot water heater is less expensive than purchasing an instant, coil-heated furnace, otherwise referred to as a "tankless water heater." Over time, however, the reduced costs of not keeping a full tank of water heated 24/7 will keep money in the owner's pocket. Having to pay more upfront to purchase a tankless water heater makes both environmental and economic sense. As green technologies continue to develop rapidly and scale up, it is reasonable to assume that costs of green materials will drop significantly. Already, the cost of solar panels has fallen appreciably.

LIMITED SELECTION

After cost, the second element preventing more people from going green is selection—or more accurately, the lack of it. Only 10 percent of the existing product supply is considered to be truly green (as opposed to those that claim to be so as a marketing tactic). In some instances, if you want to go green with a product, such as insulation, your choices will number exactly one. This insulation consists of cotton from recycled denim and costs 30 percent more than the pink stuff. It's a hard sell because after the wall is closed, nobody sees those old blue jean fibers. If builders had a greater selection of green insulation, they might be more inclined to use it. Again, there is every expectation that this will soon change. Soon, a wider variety of green products and materials will be available, due to consumer demand. You, the designer, can add your voice to the cry. Ask your sources which products are sustainable, and complain if the answer is "none." For now, green building and designing may be a bit more costly and a bit more inconvenient, but living under melt from the Arctic icecap isn't especially convenient, either.

THE DESIGNER'S RESPONSIBILITY

I firmly believe that as designers it is our responsibility to keep urging our clients to choose green products and materials. While they are often more expensive initially, green products are healthier for people and the environment and will definitely pay for themselves over time. Today and for the foreseeable future, knowledge about green practices and products can pay off handsomely for designers. Jamie Drake, one of my New York City clients, recently spoke to me about two current projects: one public, one private, both green. He writes, "These projects have helped me learn more and more about the intricacies of eco-friendly design and are giving us the expertise and tools to bring green design to many of our projects, residential as well as contract."

One of these projects is for the government of New York City. "It involves the renovation of a 1928 space. Designing under the guidelines of PlaNYC 2030, an innovative program that focuses on land, water, air, energy, and transportation with the goal of reducing global warming emissions by 30 percent, we are utilizing green materials, such as harvested stone, working with the building's existing architectural elements, applying Benjamin Moore's Aura collection of low-VOC paints, and installing eco-friendly flooring and textiles. All lighting for the renovation is in compliance with PlaNYC's goals of reduced energy, through the use of high-efficiency luminaries and lamps."

The second project is for a private philanthropic organization. "All elements of design and construction will be in accordance with LEED Gold Standards for certification. While going for a Gold Standard might seem like an Olympian task, it is often easier to achieve than expected. By utilizing wood from well-managed forests certified in accordance with the rules of the Forest Stewardship Council, (FSC), low- or non-VOC coatings and sealants, recycled glass, and LEED certified textiles, we can easily achieve our goals of Gold Standard certification."

Acronyms, acronyms, acronyms! VOC stands for "Volatile Organic Compounds," which are emitted as gases from products and may have short-term or long-term adverse health effects on people (*www.epa.gov/iaq/voc.html*). The word "volatile" alone is enough to scare me. Keep in mind that paints, carpeting, and many other indoor surfaces can give off emissions that are up to ten times more concentrated than they'd be outdoors. Think of that freshly painted nursery you designed for that nice young family—and be glad you chose low-VOC paint.

Chapter 12: THE INTERNET

❖

In my opinion, nothing has influenced the interior design industry as much as the Internet. Almost overnight, the playing field once known as "to the trade" has been leveled. Now you may protest that you shop exclusively at design centers and sources that still are "to the trade," but much of the designer mystique has been dissipated by the availability of product to anyone with an Internet connection. There has been a paradigm shift in our industry, and it is here to stay.

During presentations I have made throughout the country, designers have bemoaned the fact that their clients are sometimes finding the exact items that the designers have proposed to them on the Internet, and much less expensively at company Web sites or on eBay—brand new. When this happens, the designer, embarrassed, usually just lets the client order the merchandise and waives any commission. More often, the client finds *similar* items on the Internet and then implies that their designer is overcharging them. This is, of course, not the case from a professional perspective, but we have to deal with that ever-present perception issue.

THE EDUCATED CONSUMER

Since the advent of the Internet, consumers are more aware of their options and have become more educated and astute. Designers have two options: they can embrace this reality or they can fight it. By accepting the situation, a designer can direct their clients, setting appropriate expectations for what is and is not possible with the Internet. You, the designer, the expert in all project-related matters, need to have a conversation with your clients about the Internet and issues of reputation, quality, service, style, price, and delivery. This is actually a great conversation to have because you will learn how savvy your client really is. It is also worthwhile to discuss the positive and negative experiences they have had with Internet purchases—and your own experiences buying online.

REPUTATION

If the vendor is not already a recognized brand with previously established "bricks and mortar" stores (like Sears, Williams & Sonoma, or Pottery Barn), you cannot assume that what you see in the picture is what you will be getting. Pictures are marketing tools and can be enhanced to make the product look better than it really is. This becomes a quality issue.

QUALITY

I recently purchased a headboard and bed frame over the Internet. I don't recall the site, but the products were manufactured in China. I was pleased when I opened the package; the basic external construction and quality were excellent, and I congratulated myself on getting a great frame at a great price. Soon, my joy faded. Several holes that needed to be used to connect the frame to the headboard were not correctly sized for the provided bolts, leaving me fighting to get them to work and not securing the frame at all. After a little struggle, I managed to attach headboard to bed frame. One evening a few weeks later, while I was watching TV, several of the slats that held up the mattress suddenly broke, creating a hole into which the mattress, me, and my startled guest began to fall. Apparently, the slat wood had too many knots in it to hold the weight of a king size mattress and two occupants. This necessitated a trip to the hardware store for more slats. I also needed to get blocks to raise the mattress. The mattress fit too snugly into the frame, and it was nearly impossible to tuck in the sheets and blankets while making the bed. I needed to permanently elevate the mattress so the bed could be made. All of this required more purchases and many hours. My globally sourced "discount" headboard and bed frame ended up being not such a great deal after all.

SERVICE

No matter whom the vendor may be, problems can arise. Your clients should not assume that vendors from whom they are ordering are going to deliver the same type of service as a regular store or a trade resource with whom you, the designer, have a long-term relationship. If your clients are forced to communicate with the store by e-mail exclusively, they should beware. There will be many rounds of communications to get any matter resolved, if, indeed, it is resolved at all. If there is a phone number, encourage your clients to try using it before they order, just to see what kind of attention they receive *before* they become customers. Make sure your clients know that being a one-off customer of a Web site is not the same as being a long-term client of a vendor that values the relationship and will bend over backwards to make things right.

Style

What you see is what you get … or is it? Nothing beats being able to touch, feel, sit on, and try out whatever it is that you want to buy. I have often seen ads for tempting items that lured me into a store. Once there, I usually change my mind, because when I see or touch the item, it is just not quite right. If you are buying a large piece of furniture that does not have detailed shots from every angle, you may not be getting adequate representation of the merchandise. Let's say it's a sofa. Upon receiving it, you may decide you don't like it, after all; the arms are not quite wide enough to provide the extra "party seating" you'd envisioned.

Delivery

Now, try returning that Internet-ordered sofa, and see how easy it is to repackage it and ship it to the vendor. And don't forget about that RMA. Return Merchandise Authorization (RMA) is the number you need to place on most return shipments so that the vendor does not reject your package, once shipped—assuming that they do give you the authorization to return it. (They don't always.)

Shipping and handling are the hidden expenses that people sometimes ignore. I cringe when I get a shipping charge of $7-$10 on a small item that arrives in an envelope with $1.05 postage.

Price and Commission

While the stated price may be exceptionally good, it is not always indicative of the final price, especially when you must make modifications to the item, as I had to do with my bed frame. And you must always add on that shipping and handling charge.

When you talk to your clients about ordering from the Internet, let them know which items are truly suitable for Internet purchase.

Certain items, such as bed linens and dishware, are better priced and more convenient to order online. Others—such as furniture, non-branded items, and art—are not.

As to the issue of commission, you are entitled to whatever compensation is outlined in your agreement, so be prepared to enforce it. The Internet is just one of the many resources you may use for a project. I recommend establishing guidelines for merchandise that is acceptable for your clients to source and the types of vendors that can be trusted. You might say, "Feel free to order the pattern we agreed upon directly from Villeroy and Boch." There is also the matter of custom versus commodity. The usual reason why a price is very low is because the merchandise is not unique or made to order but is made by the thousands. While a mass-market sofa can be acceptable and even desirable, it needs to be recognized for what it is.

THE EMPOWERED DESIGNER

While the Internet has created certain challenges for today's interior designers, it has also created astonishing opportunities by giving them a way to promote their businesses to a global market. An unknown artist living in the Catskill Mountains who paints exquisite scenes on eggshells can now sell her work to collectors in Shanghai. A small design firm that specializes in chandeliers can attract clients in Paris and Dubai. All they need is a good Web site.

Through their Web sites, designers can create online portfolios and lead-generating tools for their businesses. In fact, I consider a Web site to be fundamental, and much more important than a business card, for the design professional. Surprisingly, at a recent talk (in August 2008), I queried my audience and learned that a full third of the attendees didn't have Web sites. To me, having a Web site is like having a Social Security Number: essential to everyone.

It's important that your site has a name that is easy to say and spell—not, say, Xyphex Designs. I often find myself providing my Web site address to people over the phone, and I can hear them typing it into their computers and pulling up my company information as we speak. Business happens in real time, and editors, colleagues, and potential clients can (and do) refer to Web sites during phone conversations. Their calling up your Web site is an easy way to expedite the selling process. You can get feedback and have an opportunity to respond to it before your prospect moves onto the next call, project, or whatever. Having a Web site keeps you in front of people not only during your conversation but later, whenever they want.

For those of you who have yet to build a site, I know what you will say. You will argue that you don't have the time to build a site and don't have the photographs to upload to it and don't have the money to pay a Webmaster and keep the site online. These are valid concerns. Now, ignore them. You need a Web site, and you have some options.

TIME OR MONEY?

Which do you have more of: time or money? If the answer is time, take a day and design your own Web site with the templates supplied by Internet providers such as Yahoo! (*www.yahoo.com*). Now your Web site might not look as good as a Web site created just for you by a graphic designer, but it is surely better than no Web site at all. It's quite astonishing that the average person, with no programming skills whatsoever, can create a functional Web site and publish to the World Wide Web. You can even receive mail at the site you create. What a miracle! Take a minute to admire what you've done.

Now that you've patted yourself on the back, do yourself a favor and hire a Web designer. Your self-created site might be functional, but it will not be wonderful, and since you are offering design services, you want every aspect of your marketing to look great. Potential clients might decide, "If she can't even design a beautiful Web site, I'm not going to let her design my new condo." If you hire the right firm, you will get a superb Web site with minimal hassle. You should expect some back and forth with your Web designer, who is not a mind-reader. Creating a Web site is a collaborative process, and you will be asked which colors, fonts, and designs you prefer.

YOUR WEB SITE DESIGNER

Since your Web site is going to be the centerpiece of your marketing strategy, you should hire a firm that's done work you love, so do a little research. Much like interior designers, graphic and Web designers have their own looks to which they typically adhere. While they can mimic other styles, they will lean in a particular direction if given the opportunity. So, explore the sites they've already created to see if you share their aesthetics. Next, examine the functionality (or "architecture," in Web parlance) of the sites. Do you like the way the pages flow? Are they easy to navigate? Is the content laid out in a logical manner? Can you easily get back to the home page? Whatever content you provide should be easy to read and easy to locate. Here are a few good examples of Web sites: Philip Gorrivan (*www.philipgorrivan.com*), diSalvo Interiors (*www.disalvointeriors.com*), and Design Management Company (*www.dmcnyc.com*).

After you select your Web design firm, you will probably be asked to fill out a survey of your needs and interests so that your designer can understand how to structure your site and to get a sense of the look and feel you are trying to capture. Typically, you should provide your existing stationery and logo—if you like them—so that the site will be consistent with the identity you have already created. However, if you are ready for a change, it's a great time to change everything in one fell swoop.

You will also be asked to provide the basic "content" of the site—preferably electronically, so that it can be easily configured by the designer. This content includes information about you (biography), your firm, staff, projects, awards, photography, press coverage you have received, and other resources that you wish to share, including secure access to current client project information, links to vendors you work with (architects, contractors), and information on how you work (the process of design). While this may sound daunting, you probably have most of this written and just need to pull it together. Much of this might already be in your media kit. The designer will clean things up and make your site look terrific.

Photography for Your Web Site

Of the items that I listed under content, photography is usually the stumbling block. Since we've already addressed photography in chapter 4, I will not go into it extensively here. However, it is worth noting that you can begin your site with a single project, as long as you have good photography. Even if you have only one project that is well photographed, it can tell an impressive story about the work that you do. Then, you can augment those images with others as you complete them.

I recently spoke with Susan, a designer from Cleveland who's been talking to me about doing a Web site for over a year now. She is a very successful designer and has recognized the value of a Web site, but keeps saying that she is too busy to work on one. Fortunately, I decided to follow my own sales advice and probe more deeply into the objection by discussing the process involved with developing a site. I told her that it typically doesn't take too much time to pull together the needed materials. But it turned out that Susan had no current photography—although she had six projects that need to be photographed. In her case, "too busy" translated into "worried about the expense of photography." She also wasn't sure that local photographers could capture the essence of her work. I was able to pair her up with a New York photographer who does exceptional interiors work and provides volume discounts. There is usually a match out there for most relationships; you just need to find a good matchmaker.

ORGANIZING YOUR WEB SITE

Make sure your site is straightforward, with tabs that take people where they need to go, right away. Your homepage should have your logo and a color scheme that will be consistent throughout the site. It should have a "money shot" of your work—one large image that you feel really defines who you are and that is inviting; you want to draw people into your site. You will then provide a tab to your "about us" section, which contains information about you, your company, and your staff. You will also have a "portfolio" section, which will contain images of your work. I do not think it is necessary to label the sections according to rooms (i.e., kitchen, living rooms, etc.), as it is usually obvious to the viewer. However, if you have work in multiple specialties—residential, commercial, and hospitality, for example— then you should group them into separate sections. It's always good to have a "resources" page, which contains links to your favorite vendors, publications you read and recommend, or just about anything that shows you are informed. A "pressroom" will contain your publicity, which can include covers of publications and the actual text of stories written about your projects, as well as articles you have written yourself. If you write a newsletter, a "library" page can archive current and back issues.

If you are going to keep and maintain a blog, you will need a tab for that as well. A blog is a contraction of the term "Web log"; it's a public diary maintained by an individual with regular entries. Many blogs provide commentary or news on a particular subject; others function as more personal online diaries. A typical blog combines text, images, and links to other blogs, Web pages, and other media related to its topic. The ability for readers to leave comments in an interactive format is an important part of many blogs. I recommend that you only have a blog if you are willing to contribute to it at least once a week, with a paragraph or more, so that it stays relevant and you satisfy returning visitors by providing new content. Speaking from my own experience, it is challenging to factor this into your schedule when there are so many other things to which you must attend, such as, let us not forget, *design.*

KEEPING IT CURRENT

A Web site is like a resume—always a work in progress. Keep your Web site current by adding new documents, updating links, uploading images, and posting press releases or text-heavy portfolio additions to engage viewers and turn them into repeat visitors. Make it a point to update your Web site at least once a month, ideally adding a new section, adjusting the overall design of a page, or enhancing existing features, from blog postings and background music to widgets or downloadable content. Each time you update your Web site, you might have to enlist the help your web designer, which could get expensive. So, before the Web designer starts creating your site, make it clear that you want to be able to make minor changes and updates on your own.

YOUR ONLINE STORE

An online store, if is part of your Web site, can change its dynamics and cost. Whether or not you have a retail store with a physical presence, you can display and sell products online through a "store." You will need to determine if you are going to transact purchases on your site or if clients need to contact you in order to place a sale. If you want the site to be fully automated, you will need to accept credit cards and establish secure transaction processing on your site, both of which can cost over $1,000 to set up and then require monthly maintenance fees, whether or not you sell a single item. Still, if you do a lot of volume, an online store can provide a nice income stream.

HTML and Flash

Your Web designer will have expertise in HTML and Flash, the two essentials in building Web pages. HTML (or "Hypertext Markup Language") provides the means to determine the structure of text-based information in a document by denoting certain text as links, headings, paragraphs, lists, and so on—and to supplement that text with interactive forms, and embedded images. Flash has become a popular method for adding animation and interactivity to Web pages. In short, text is usually written in HTML, and movement (pictures that rotate or appear as slideshows) are written in Flash. Your site must be largely HTML in order for potential clients to find it when searching for firms with your skill set.

Search Engine Optimization

Most people are familiar with Google and Yahoo!—perhaps the best known of the various "engines" used to conduct searches of information. If you want to buy a sofa in your neighborhood, you might type "contemporary sofas in Chelsea, New York" and get a listing of the various stores that carry contemporary sofas, as long as those stores have put the key words "contemporary" and "sofa" and "Chelsea" in the HTML text of their Web sites. If the Webmaster used Flash to write the text, the search engines will not find it and will not display that store as an option. The same holds true for a designer's Web site and the many keywords that designers might use, such as "interior design," "antiques," "project management," "accessories," etc. If you and your Web designer plan incorrectly, you will miss out on business you might otherwise have gotten.

There is a whole segment of the Web industry that is devoted to Search Engine Optimization (SEO), which improves your rank in search engine results. You can be charged anywhere from a few hundred dollars to a few thousand to have your site optimized. This ensures that when someone types in keywords that you have in your site, your site appears high in the list of results. As in the offline world, a business is only successful if consumers can find it. Consumers should be able to easily find your Web site based on industry-specific keywords. As a rule, you want to be on the first page of results, or at least on the second. Most people do not go beyond two pages (or often even the first few results). Your goal is to get your site into the top five listings of any particular design category.

If you really expect to generate new business from just your Web site, you must establish reciprocal links to score highly with the search engines. Whenever someone mentions your name or your business on a Web page, try to get them to put up an active link to your Web site as well. These active links, also referred to as reciprocal links between two sites, will give you greater credibility with search engines, which will push you up in keyword search results. A high ranking on a Google search is a huge help to a designer. If you can't achieve that, consider a sponsored link on Google. This is a "paid search ad," and can also get you a lot of clicks, but watch out—you'll pay for each of those clicks, even if none gets converted to a lead. Luckily, you can establish a limit. Google has changed how advertising works (along with so much else). You can pay for a limited number of clicks (say, $500 worth) and then have the ad withdrawn.

Online Ads

If you want to promote your Web site (and business) online, you can promote it through online advertising. Where might you advertise? The best idea is to buy space on related sites that attract your desired demographic. You might consider advertising on your local e-newsletter or on the commercial Web site for your town. If your specialty is children's rooms, consider placing ads on a parenting site; if your expertise is aging-in-place, investigate the type of healthy living sites that seniors often visit.

Banner, Skyscraper, and Square Ads

Banner ads are the old stalwart of the Web. These are horizontal ads at the top or bottom of a Web site. While these ads are ubiquitous, traditionally they do not have a very high click-through rate. Of course, click-through rate and conversion (to leads) are entirely dependent upon the quality of the ad, the accurate placement on synergistic media properties, and the call to action within their message. Ranges vary from .001 to as high as 20 percent, with most toward the lower end. As these metrics are dependent upon multiple variables, there is no meaningful average figure. Skyscraper ads are similar to banner ads, but instead of running across the screen horizontally, they are vertical. They, too, are better for branding than for selling. Square ads are generally placed in the middle of a screen and break up the text in a Web site.

Pop-Ups, Pop-Unders and Others

No doubt you are familiar with those irritating ads that pop up in a new window over the site you are reading. While these ads are generally unwelcome, and there are several pop-up blockers that prevent most of them from appearing, people do persist in designing and paying for them because these ads have a relatively high click-through rate. But pop-ups are a dying breed, as nearly all new computers are being built with blocking software. This applies to pop-unders as well. As the name implies, pop-unders are similar to pop-ups, but they open underneath the current Web page. You won't know they are there until after you click off the window you're viewing and they suddenly manifest themselves. Their click-through rate is slightly less than for pop-up ads. There are also interstitial ads, which appear after you click an internal site and before the new site loads. Overlays are ads that will overtake the background of the site you are looking at by replacing, overwriting it, or hovering around the screen. Sounds annoying, doesn't it?

More innovative types of advertising are coming into existence as the Web matures, so this is not meant to be an exhaustive list. However, it covers all the main types of advertising in use today. I will not address pricing, since it varies so much, but suffice it to say you can make a full-time job just trying to figure it out. Should you decide to advertise, decide how you will measure the success of your campaign. Are you looking for more hits to your Web site or calls to your firm, or do you only want actual interviews with potential clients?

RESOURCES

Two software programs have been created for the interior designer: Studio Designer and Design Manager. Soon, they will offer Web interfaces that allow your clients to check on the status of their projects at any time. They can see where orders are in processing, look at notes you may have left for them, and view photos specific to their project that you have uploaded to the site. This is useful for clients who always want to be in touch or overseas clients who are in different time zones and need access at times that may not convenient for your office. While I think that this will become more prevalent in the future, as clients start demanding it, at present most designers do not want this kind of scrutiny from their clients.

Who, in the end, benefits from the Internet: your client, who can source from the globe, or you, who can market to the world? The answer is both of you. Talk about a win-win situation.

Chapter *13:* LICENSING

❖

Name recognition is marketing's penultimate goal (the ultimate goal, of course, being the purchase of a product or service). Your hope is that when potential clients need to hire interior designers, they will think of you at the precise moment they are ready to make that call. Major corporations have spent billions of dollars on marketing so that you think of their brand first when you are ready to fly, eat fast food, drink beer, and buy running shoes—anything and everything.

The design industry also has preeminent brands that designers and consumers think of when they shop. Ethan Allen, Ralph Lauren, and Martha Stewart are all recognizable in the home furnishings industry. As for designers, consumers might know Thom Felicia, Barbara Barry, and Joe Ruggiero, while trade professionals would definitely recognize Thomas Pheasant, Michael Berman, Jamie Drake, and Clodagh. These designers each have their own product lines, and their name recognition is a valuable commodity in selling those goods.

THE CELEBRITY SELL

Most people are familiar with licensing from consumer goods that bear the name of a celebrity on some product he or she probably didn't design but about which we trust their authority. Take my Jack LaLanne juicer. While Jack probably did not engineer the machine, I know him as a fitness guru, and if he endorses the product, it's probably good. The same concept applies to home furnishings. If Jamie Drake likes a particular fabric, he probably uses it in his projects, and since I like his work and he is acknowledged to be talented by the media, then the product must also be good. But what comes first—the name or the fame; the product line or the recognition? It's hard to say. Fame and name feed each other, and a successful product line can certainly help your design business—and vice versa. But are you ready to consider licensing? Perhaps not (yet), but consider this option for the future.

Most designers I know have designed custom pieces of furniture or accessories, sometimes out of desire and often out of necessity—they just can't find what they are looking for in the market. Once they have a few pieces in their portfolio, they consider producing the furniture because they think it will appeal to their peers. This presents them with two options: produce and distribute the furniture themselves or find a manufacturer that will do it for them. Option two is the best, since there is a tremendous amount of time involved with creating proto- types, manufacturing product, marketing it, distributing it, and selling it. In fact, so much time is involved that option two is usually not avail- able unless the manufacturer can be assured that the collection will sell. What usually convinces the manufacturer? Name recognition.

NAME RECOGNITION

There are a number of ways people can obtain name recognition out- side the design industry per se and then leverage it to their advan- tage. Television is one source; for example, shows like *Queer Eye for the Straight Guy* and *Trading Spaces.* The actors were associated with décor and developed their names with the mass market as a result of the exposure. Thom Felicia of *Queer Eye* has gone on to create a very successful interior design career for himself. Then there is the Hollywood machine that is churning out stars who want a piece of the home market, including Jaclyn Smith, who licenses her eponymous collection through Hickory Hill Furniture and other companies. And who says you need to be alive to sell furniture? Walt Disney and Humphrey Bogart have collections, too. Next, you have tastemakers like Chris Madden and B. Smith entering the fray. There is also the crossover between fashion and interiors, as celebrated by publications like *Elle Décor* and exemplified by designers like Vera Wang, Kate Spade, Todd Oldham, and Ralph Lauren. In addition, there are historic places that have captured attention and space in American homes including Colonial Williamsburg, Newport Mansions, and Winterthur. Being highly decorated (published) by the editors in our industry might also help get your work licensed.

After reading all the names in the last paragraph, you might be asking yourself if there is still room to add more names and product to the market. The answer is yes, of course. There is always room in the market for a unique collection that has a clear product story and a target customer. On the flipside, a "name" will not save a weak licensing concept or poor design. If the product isn't good, it's not going to sell.

Working the Steps

Taking a product to market and having it sell is not an easy task. If you want to give this a go, here are the steps you will need to follow:

1. Choose the category you are targeting.

Furniture	Textiles
Contract Furnishings	Window Hardware

Outdoor Furniture	Window Treatments
Wall Covering	Bathroom Fixtures & Tiles
Tabletop & Dinnerware	Bathroom Accessories
Giftware	Decorative Accessories
Hardware	Soft Accessories
Carpet	Paper products
Rugs	Retail

2. Decide how you are going to position your offering: is there going to be a celebrity component or will you be a behind-the-scenes designer? It is possible to find a manufacturer that will produce your designs without promoting your name. They may be looking to develop a collection and have their own brand to promote (think Ethan Allen). If you want your name to be involved, then you'll have to look for a new deal.

3. Determine the theme of your collection. (It has to be based on more than just good design.) Then, create marketing materials to support the theme that will be used in your pitch. Remember that you'll be pitching manufacturers, not consumers. Your target market—manufacturers—may find your wit and glamour irrelevant; they just want to know that they will make a profit.

4. Research the target companies for your pitch. You need to identify the manufacturers that you will approach to develop your property. This is harder than it may seem since there are so many good manufacturers, both nationally and internationally.

5. Once you identify some desirable companies, try to understand their needs. See if they are missing something in their current product offering that you can provide, and then develop rapport

with the key decision makers—all of them. You need to know with whom you are dealing; specifically, their titles, roles, and authority. People may leave a company or change positions, and you will need to pick up the pieces with a replacement, so relationship development with the licensee is crucial.

6. Negotiate your deal. This can take a few months to a year, depending upon the company, the scope of the offering, and the skill of your negotiator.

7. Develop the product. Once you've signed your deal, you will work with the company, providing the concept designs and prototype development through the manufacturing of the finished product. You will probably need to make factory visits to check on quality and execution.

Work With the Pros

This entire process will go much more smoothly if you work with professionals who understand the business and the players. There is only a handful of good ones that I have encountered over the last ten years, and they are always at the major shows around the world, maintaining crucial relationships and forging new ones. The playing field is constantly changing, and you need to find someone who is actively involved in meeting manufacturers and structuring deals to serve as your business agent. (My friend and colleague Gerg Vargo in New York is a great resource.)

Will you get rich or famous from a licensing deal? Probably not, but hopefully, the deal will be structured in a profitable manner, the collection will actually sell, and you will receive proceeds from the manufacturer. However, it is not uncommon for designers to go through this process just for the exposure it will bring them. It takes so much money to manufacture and distribute furniture that there may not be much left over for you unless the collection is a smash hit. I know of one prominent New York designer who had a fabric collection with a vendor who is no longer in business. When I asked about his sales figures for that year, he replied, with comic precision, "$678.15." That same designer now has many profitable collections with mainstream manufacturers; he used that initial foray as a stepping stone in his career. The marketing of his first collection benefited the designer and further developed his name recognition.

Speaking of marketing, both marketing and sales distribution are the responsibility of the licensee (manufacturer). The vendor will decide on the advertising, promotional materials, location of showrooms, sales representatives, customer service, and everything required to actually get product to market. It is important that you are specific about how you will be referenced in the marketing materials and that you find out in advance exactly what will be done to market the collection. Even when you do negotiate well, you need to check to make sure that the manufacturer lives up to its part of the bargain. One of my clients was supposed to be listed as the designer of the furniture collection in all advertising, but was not. We brought this to the manufacturer's attention, and the designer received the credit that was due.

The process of licensing your line will take a great deal of time and money, and you could very well end up without a deal. Timing is everything, and sometimes the pieces just don't fall into place. It's possible that you will not be able to agree on terms or that the money being offered is not sufficient. You may also have terrific rapport with a key decision maker who leaves and is replaced by someone who isn't keen on you or your program. It's not uncommon that during negotiations a company will be sold or go into bankruptcy, interrupting or voiding the negotiations altogether. And then there is the name game: you could be bumped by someone who enters the scene with a more prominent name or more salable concept, and since there are limited development dollars available, you are sidelined indefinitely.

Every mountain you climb takes exertion and stamina; getting to the top is the reward. If you remain interested in licensing your products, then engage a professional and give it a shot. It has worked for many people, and it could well work for you.

Chapter 14: Designers Dish it Out!

❖

To provide designers with further guidance about marketing, I interviewed several prominent interior designers to get their candid thoughts about marketing and design. I also interviewed a wealth expert to get his ideas about working with the affluent. Then, I distributed questionnaires to the attendees at one of my recent workshops and chose their most instructive and interesting answers for you to consider as you formulate your marketing plans. Dig in!

LINDA LEACH

My first client was my friend—a very patient, kind, understanding and encouraging friend. In speaking to many other designers, I have found that our best clients start out being our friends, relatives, and neighbors. Then, they were the friends of friends, and the neighbor's relatives, and thus the clientele has grown. As in most businesses, the bulk of our business is based on repeats and referrals. It takes a determined marketing effort to move beyond those early circles of relationships.

Because I entered the interior design profession as a more mature adult, I came into interior design with transferable skills. No matter what the former career or occupation, there are life lessons and skills that can be used in the new career. When I was in eighth grade, my mother made me take a typing class, stating that if I could type, I would always be able to find a job. The machinery has definitely changed, but the skills learned in that typing class have served me well. As simple as that illustration seems, we can always dust off and reuse experience in new ways.

Most business owners are ultimately salespeople. We have a service or product that we perceive has use to the public, and in return, we expect that public to provide something that we need: money. There are labor relations laws that must be applied, no matter what the industry. So, either you have had employees, have managed employees, or have been an employee and thus have some exposure or knowledge about labor relations laws.

The biggest challenge of managing my own business is cash flow. The interior design business has highs and lows of capital. When a sale is made and a deposit is collected, cash is flowing freely. However, before the product can ship, much of that product must be paid for, so cash flow is tight. Then, the final invoice is paid for by the client, and cash is freely flowing again. The trick is to manage a number of projects that are in different phases of development in order to level the peaks and valleys of cash management.

As with most small businesses, interior design firms are notoriously under-capitalized. A good business manager keeps a watch of all expenditures and carefully controls overhead expenses. The basics of business management are "sales less cost equals profit." This means that the creative, artistic interior designer who owns and manages his or her own firm must be the outside salesperson as well as the meticulous bookkeeper in order to create the margin that we call profit. Remember, the theory is that we can actually earn a living while using our creative gifts to create beautiful spaces.

As an occasional employer, I have read a lot of job applications from interior designers seeking employment. Most of these applicants state that one of their major strengths is the ability to "get along well with others." Interpersonal relationships are never more important than in a small design firm. Interior designers work from the heart. What we present to the public is a visible representation of what we have dreamed. Our work is very emotional.

And emotion plays a huge part in how we price our services. Unless we have an encouraging mentor or a body of experience that instills confidence, interior designers are likely to undercharge for the services that they render, sometimes from lack of self-esteem. We designers must sell ourselves on our qualifications before we can sell our public on our fees. Obtaining that degree in interior design and acquiring the appropriate licensing are two ways that the interior designer sells the value of his or her services and justifies his or her fees.

I don't like surprises and assume my clients don't like them either. I make sure that each client has a signed contract clearly defining what is expected of me, the designer, and what is expected of the client. The contract is reviewed by the designer and the client so that each clearly understands expectations. A design fee is collected for all design services, and payment is made for all products sold. A client is not reluctant to pay for services when those services are clearly defined. Even though everything is very clearly defined, a contract is basically a letter of agreement between two people of integrity. When one party has no integrity, that contract will fail.

I have also learned to collect my design fee up front, before the design process begins. People have a tendency to undervalue a designer's time and talent and can be quite proud of themselves when they take our ideas without paying for them. At the same time, I have seen way too many designers who are so excited to be involved in a particular project that they freely give away concepts for which they should be compensated. The only things a designer really has to sell are ideas. Don't be afraid to charge for them.

The clients of mine who have been most awful about paying have been attorneys. They will say, "Please bill me hourly, as that is how I also work." Somehow, an attorney feels no shame in charging me for "research time" or "phone calls," but they question the time spent when a designer does research for a project. Much of a designer's time is spent behind the scenes, fleshing out design concepts. We spend time researching products and availability. We consult with other experts concerning structural engineering or code compliance. We peruse catalogs and showrooms searching for appropriate products. We consult other designers for resources or solutions to problems. The professional interior designer needs to be compensated for this time.

I know that there are certain cultures in which "bargaining" is a big part of the game. So, if I charge for two hours of research time, a client has been known to call to negotiate for one hour of research time. If my experts tell me that a certain window treatment requires forty-two yards of fabric, a client who has no expertise in the manufacture of window treatments will determine that he should only pay for thirty-five yards of fabric. Sometimes, interior design is all about people skills.

I had a fairly developed marketing strategy when I started the business. That marketing strategy, simply stated, addressed the who, where, when, what, and how of my design world. I started out asking myself what I did best. What aspect of design brought me the greatest joy? From what part of design could I develop the greatest profit? When I figured out what I did well and what I liked to do, I was able to move to the next question, which was, Who was my market? When I knew who my market was, I needed to find out where they were. Now that I understood where they were, what was I selling them and how could I reach them to sell my services?

All the finer points of publicity and public relations were developed from the understanding of my market, what they were buying, and how I could reach them. Handing out embroidered baseball caps may not be the way to attract clientele for a firm specializing in high-end residential design. However, I still phone the same plumber every time because he gave me a magnetic business card that I keep attached to the side of the refrigerator. I may laugh at my realtor, who passes out notepads with his picture and phone number imprinted at the top. But I use that notepad every day, so when the time comes for me to use the services of a realtor, that name will be at the top of my list.

I want my dream client to think of me first when he is ready to make a design decision. I want my dream client to call me whenever she wants to make a change that involves design. What can I give that client that will remind her of my presence? One of my favorite gifts to give is a beautiful notebook for recording thoughts, with a handwritten inscription expressing my thanks for working on the project.

It is imperative for every viable design firm to develop a marketing strategy and to implement that strategy. Challenging times require a firm commitment to marketing. I love the quote from Stuart Henderson Britt, "Doing business without advertising is like winking at someone in the dark. You know what you're doing, but nobody else does."

Marketing is different from selling. Marketing is putting the face of your business before your ideal client, and giving that client the opportunity to purchase your design.

Any successful marketing strategy goes back to the two most basic questions:

1. Who is my client?

2. How can I reach that client?

Marketing is a great outlet for a creative designer. We are creative problem solvers, so we are constantly re-evaluating our marketing strategy to see what works best. What worked yesterday may not work today. Great ideas become stale with overuse.

Interior design comes with a certain perceived panache. My firm specializes in high-end residential design. My clients definitely buy into the concept of "perceived value." For instance, Tiffany has done a fabulous job of creating an icon of its name. The perception is that if it comes in a little blue box, it has to be the best. I want that same panache or icon status for my design firm. I want people to feel that if they hire Trinity Bay Interiors to do their design work, they are hiring the best. They will be able to brag to their friends that Linda Leach from Trinity Bay Interiors did their design, just as the new bride might flash her ring and boast that hers is a Tiffany diamond.

I am currently thinking that it might be nice to have a patron. Artisans in the past were sponsored by people of wealth, to enable artisans to concentrate on the highest level of art without the constraints of budget. I am thinking that a patron might be a great client.

Thank you, Lloyd, for giving me the privilege of participating in your book. Your business insights have always been very helpful to me. You are a great encourager!

Linda Leach is a designer from Newport Beach, CA, who made a mid-life career change and built a flourishing design practice. She is also an educator at the Interior Designers Institute in Newport Beach, CA.

Her interiors may be seen at www.trinitybayinteriors.com.

Benjamin Noriega-Ortiz

I got my first real client through the recommendation of a friend, and from then on, clients started coming from magazine publications, as well as from former clients. I had no idea of what a marketing strategy was when I started my business. I only knew that I had to photograph and publish as much as I could. I learned that from John Saladino, my former boss, who at the time (in the 1980s) seemed to be in every magazine every month. Now, my marketing strategy is to diversify my reach and to always keep my name out there. With experience, I have learned that having your name regularly mentioned in magazines and newspapers and now the Internet helps create a brand. This recognition has helped me gain clients and also expand into licensing projects.

The biggest challenge in managing my business has always been book-keeping and assessing how much to charge for a particular project. When we started venturing into hospitality projects, we saw that our standard hourly rate would not apply to these kinds of projects, and the challenge was to assess how much our time would be worth so that all of our creations would be money-making ventures.

Having studied architecture and worked as an architect in my early years helped a lot in establishing my style as an interior designer. However,

I feel that a previous career in marketing, law, or finance would have helped quite a bit more with the business end of it. I have done well so far, but it has been an uphill road that doesn't seem to level, ever.

I tend to under-price a job when I like either the particular job or the client. It doesn't happen often, and I have learned that there are two kinds of jobs to take: the ones that make you more money and the ones that you will publish. For the ones I know will photograph well and will give me good publicity I am always willing to "lose in order to gain." (Sometimes, when I am working on that kind of project, I have to remind myself about this.)

Almost every client is reluctant to pay for time rather than goods. Clients can also be hesitant about paying for expensive fabrics, because they might be able to get the same "look" for less money. But a luxury fabric has a different feel and value and will usually last a lot longer.

One of my dream projects has always been some sort of place of worship. I am not really religious (perhaps "spiritual" best describes me), but I consider that there is something uplifting and magical in my work that could lend itself to a spiritual experience. The closest I've gotten has been designing hotels. Creating a space that can make you think about interiors as art has always been a goal of mine, and designing hotels has taken me closer to that goal.

Benjamin Noriega-Ortiz is a designer who is known for exotic feathers and modern chic. His work is sought after by celebrities and global design gurus alike. He is no-nonsense in his approach and entirely cool in his outcome. See his rooms at www. bnodesign.com.

CHARLES GREBMEIER

I got my first client when the owner of the design studio where I worked told me that a particular person always came into the studio on Saturdays to look around. I had just completed two display windows. When the person came in, I introduced myself to her. She mentioned liking the colors chartreuse, cream, and black. We talked, and I was hired twenty minutes later. The project at retail was $60,000 (and that was in 1965!). Client one referred me to her friend, who became client as well within a few weeks.

When I first started out, I taught a design class at a junior college, lectured at the local Junior League, and spoke at women's clubs and social clubs. I was on the local lecture circuit, you might say. I opened my own studio a little later, and all that talking paid off. Now, I have a MySpace page, which has gotten me several referrals. I find that 50 percent of my time is taken up managing the business rather than designing. As well as having design skills and believing in myself, I find it very useful to surround myself with good people (like you, Lloyd).

I have undercharged my clients when I haven't billed them for the designer's trade mark-up of 40-50 percent and also when I've lowered my design-time rate below $250 per hour. Also, I realize that I should always bill $150 per hour for administration (producing sales proposals, reviewing purchase orders, confirming net pricing, tracking info from the different sources, etc.). Clients usually understand that I have to do this, but sometimes clients don't understand that it's the details that really "make" a room—i.e., additional lighting, beautiful accessories. They can be reluctant to pay for these items.

My dream client is an inventor of a special disc drive. I have designed three of his residences: a 10,000-square-foot home in Santa Cruz, a 2,500-square-foot penthouse in San Francisco, and a 15,000-square-foot house in Pebble Beach.

Charles Grebmeier has over forty years of experience and is known for his refined and elegant approach to design. Rich hues and opulent textures combined with traditional and modern elements create lived-in environments that are luxurious but unpretentious. See Charles Grebmeier's work at www.designfinder.com/grebmeier *and* www. grebmeierdesign.com.

EMILY CASTLE

My first client was a referral from an architect friend of mine. Once she realized how I could take her plans and see the job through to completion, the referrals kept coming. My degree in architecture allows me to work seamlessly with architects and contractors. My ideas are more readily accepted by clients and professionals because of my advanced education.

I did not have a strategy in the beginning, other than to do the very best job I could to start to develop a following. I knew that my reputation meant everything. Today, I have a storefront office with great exposure, an informative Web site, ad contracts with print media, and word of mouth referrals. The combination provides me with more work than I can handle, and I can be selective about the jobs I take.

Early on, I took on a project that had unfamiliar aspects, and my lack of confidence stopped me from charging what I was worth. It was crazy, since I knew that I would do the extra research to bring myself up to speed on any detail. Now I charge what I'm worth, but I never ask for that final payment until my clients are totally satisfied.

One of my challenges has been having people work under my firm name doing their own design. I have had one good experience with this situation but am hesitant about accepting others.

Right now, I am in designer heaven. I am working on a house with a fine architect, an award-winning kitchen designer, a landscape architect, and a lighting designer. Truly the best team you could put together in our area, and I am pleased to be a part of it. The project will span the next two years, and I will oversee all aspects. The client appreciates my ability to balance the egos of other professionals while providing them with an integrated first-class interior design.

Emily Castle is a trained architect and interior designer who brings her warm and energetic personality to create similar interiors. See her work at www.emilycastle.com.

BRUCE LONG

When I opened my own business, a newspaper profiled me and wrote about my previous experience. My first client called right away, and said, "Anyone who worked for Mark Hampton, I want." The second, third, and so on have been word of mouth.

The biggest challenge of managing my own business has been staffing. It is very time-consuming and difficult finding people who have a strong work ethic, fit into the office "family," share my design philosophy, and have talent to boot. Only the need for cash flow has made me under-price my services, and it doesn't happen often. I've found that clients are sometimes reluctant to pay for things that aren't tangible "rewards," such as state tax, delivery charges, or hourly administrative fees.

I've had a number of ideal clients. They love design, they have great personal style, and they are enthusiastic and open to new ideas. They do not equate style with cost and vice-versa. Their most important quality? They have trust. Plus, they pay their bills, are patient about waiting for what they want, and are truly appreciative.

Bruce Long is a prominent residential designer in Princeton, NJ and New York City. See his work at www.bnl-interiordesign.com.

KRIS KOLAR

Regardless of price point, stores are trying to add interior designers to staff to capture the high-end customer. At a certain echelon, people require the level of service and sophistication that comes from trained professionals, something beyond what can be delivered by the regular selling staff. As a result of this hiring trend, "old-guard" practicing designers are struggling with their businesses, losing some clients to the retail stores and not capturing as much of a project as they might hope.

Here at Robb & Stucky, our philosophy is that interior design services are who we are and what we do. Our business is usually not about selling one piece of furniture: we build on the sale, asking how big the room is, and what else is in the room. We think of ourselves as large design studios that happen to be attached to large showrooms. It is interior designers who have made Robb & Stucky the organization that it is today.

As a whole, the design industry has lost some of its luster, particularly in the realm of "to the trade." Design centers are now admitting the public, democratizing the once-privileged domain of interior design profession-als. And while access does not instill talent, it does remove some of the mystery. As consumers have gained access, they have often made expen-sive mistakes by purchasing on their own. Of course, with every cloud, there is a silver lining—they then realize the value of design service.

Cable television shows like those on HGTV have also affected the field by raising consumer expectations. The shows make it appear as if a room miraculously comes together in an hour, without paying homage to the creative and installation teams that are behind the scenes, working for days to make a room glamorous.

In reality, designers save customers considerable time through their technical knowledge. Designers bring scale and proportion to a space through the proper selection of furniture and finishes. In today's hectic world, time is our most precious commodity, and now more than ever, a home needs to be a refuge. Clients do not have time to shop all over to find the ideal accent lamp, the right style sofa, or the perfect slab of granite. What an interior designer offers a client is time. Designers have the expertise to shop and present selections that will fit the style of the room and prevent costly errors.

I would say to designers, "Don't see Robb & Stucky as a competitor, but as a resource!" Because we run a $70 million inventory, we can finish up jobs with product that is in stock and ready for white-glove delivery in forty-eight states. The scale of rooms is different in the Sun Belt, with ceilings being significantly higher and rooms often being larger, and when designers come from other states, they sometimes misjudge the amount or size of furniture they will need. So, they run to us at R & S and add what is necessary to fill out a project. We also have an extensive fabric library, which designers are free to browse and from which they can place orders for our merchandise.

We are like a department store of furnishings, with many styles and price points. Because mid-range product wasn't easily available, we created our own private label.

Today, there is a crossover between residential and hospitality special-ties. People want a retreat when they travel, and hotels are seeking residential designers to give rooms that feel. Many residential designers see hospitality as a way to quick riches if they do the right project that gets widespread attention. However, designing a hotel is different from designing a house and requires special training, so it's not necessarily an easy transition. An easier transition is designing timeshares: vacation ownership properties that will be used by others. These properties must strike the right balance between individuality and impersonality; the owner's collection of African weapons might not be on the walls, but vacationing strangers don't want a sterile environment, either.

Many members of our design team are hired right out of design school and serve as assistants to established designers here before generating their own client base. Others are senior designers that have their own design businesses. Designers at Robb & Stucky basically run their own design business under our umbrella. Theirs are the names on the projects.

Kris Kolar is Vice President of Design at Robb & Stucky, the largest highend interior design firm in the country, employing more than 1,300 people at thirty facilities.

LEWIS SCHIFF

There is a time for discretionary luxury and a time for more restrained luxury. The culture sways back and forth. Even within one family unit, there may be more of an emphasis on status by one family member and functionality by another. It is the designer's job to sort out these competing points of view and create a solution that fits everyone's needs—or at least fits them as well as possible. In this regard, a designer's job transcends that of a creative professional and moves into that of an "advisor" or a "support provider."

Think of your role as helping the busy family solve problems and realizing their vision for living—one that is rooted in their personal tastes and capable of practical implementation. How you fit this role is likely to be the difference between being a successful designer and a struggling designer. In other words, relationships matter. With your best clients, you'll be "in relationship"—you'll understand them and guide them toward solutions that meet their conflicting needs of taste, budget, and the combined personalities of the players. You'll guide them not toward what he wants but what *they* want. Discovering, acknowledging, and satisfying this third entity ("they") is what is meant by being "in relationship" with your clients.

Only the best of us can do this with any regularity. For most of us, this is a new skill set. I describe this role as being part of your client's "Circle of Support," wherein you accept that your job is to help them using your skills so they can go on and do their job (raising a family, being an accountant, etc.). Positioning yourself as a problem solver or a trusted advisor to a smaller, more focused clientele is a likely path to long-term success in any profession and any market. For many, this prescription is a challenge because it calls on you to develop a full complement of business development and relationship skills. Successfully achieving this will take you beyond being a practitioner and turn you into a businessperson.

If it's your goal to succeed professionally and not just creatively, you'll need to bring these new skills to the table. In addition, we know that hard work, networking skills, and perseverance—even when times are difficult—are universal characteristics of most successful people. This is no different for the designer. Left brain? Right brain? A little bit of both. The marketplace calls on us to deliver excellence in so many ways in order to succeed that it's unrealistic to rely on our strengths and not consider what dormant talents lie beneath.

There are two exceptions to this path of hard work and skill-building that I've described. First, you can be enormously talented—a visionary whose time comes while you're still vital and able to enjoy it. Second, you can get extremely lucky in any number of ways that catapult you to success. Perhaps you are lucky. Perhaps you do have enormous talent. Still, there's little one can do to maximize these. Instead, focus on the areas you can control. As golf champion Gary Player once said, "The more I practice, the luckier I get."

When marketing to the new affluent, meaning the 70 percent of wealthy households who have made their wealth rather than inherited it, it's essential to understand that they represent an amalgam of both their old and new worlds. Their values were, in most instances, solidified in the house they grew up in. If this is one of the scores of millions of middle-class households that were the hallmark of the latter half of the twentieth century, they likely have the same values that we've come to understand by watching the television sitcom: a commitment to family, to education, to "a day's work for a day's pay," and a goal of a white-collar job or management position.

However, consider that most of today's self-made wealthy create their fortunes through private business ownership. Are these folks the same as the rest of the middle class? Not likely. We call them "high-capacity individuals" because our research suggests that they are able to reach higher heights than most of us, particularly in areas of hard work (working seventy hours per week on average), perseverance (failing more often professionally because that's the way they learn), networking (reporting knowing more people and knowing more about those people than most of us) and a keen sense of their goal: to be financially independent.

While most of us can claim some of these skills, the nation's "Middle-Class Millionaires" simply do it better. As a part of the Middle-Class Millionaire's support system, designers need to understand the way their clients' middle-class values weave together with their exceptional skills in wealth creation. This is key to delivering on the promise for them. They care most of all about two things: family and business. To a much lesser extent do they care about friendships (which are different from "relationships") or hobbies or even commitments to their communities. They are keenly focused on their two most important goals (family and business) and any practitioner that hopes to win their business disregards this reality at their own peril.

How can you help them be successful in these two areas of life? There are a number of ways, including understanding their commitment to family and how that can reveal itself. I've known many families that install basketball and racquetball courts in their homes. Are these status symbols or a way to keep their families together? Does this help them succeed in the workplace? Or does it help them stay in shape to enjoy longevity for the benefit of their children and grandchildren? Understanding the motivation behind their actions will allow you to serve them best.

In addition, be advised that having two all-important life goals, work and family, is very time-demanding. The Middle-Class Millionaire is the most time-challenged segment of the population. If you waste their time, you won't be of use to them very long. Understanding how they want to work with you is key to successfully serving them. Do they want you to make all the decisions or do they want to know the ins and outs of the way you work? Do they want to communicate with you efficiently over e-mail, or do they want you to join them for relaxed conversations when it's convenient for them? There is no single answer to these and other questions. As you serve them, you'll come to appreciate that flexibility in being in relationship with them is more than just value-add: in many cases, it is the primary source of your value to them. This is why it pays to focus on a certain segment of the population. For example:

• First-generation wealth versus "old money"

• Corporate employees versus business owners

• Families versus older folks or single people

• Office or home

The most successful of us have a core focus, a group we serve best because it suits who we are and how we do business. Find yours, and you'll find the success and satisfaction you seek.

Lewis Schiff is CEO of Advanced Planning Group and co-author of The Middle-Class Millionaire *and* The Armchair Millionaire. *He is a longtime contributor to CNNMoney.com and TheStreet. com and maintains a blog about the Middle-Class Millionaire for InvestmentAdvisor.com.*

WORKSHOP PARTICIPANTS
BIGGEST CHALLENGE

"Asking for money, and having them comfortable with fees and mark-up."

—Jean Zimmas, Santa Monica, CA

"I don't see the people in this city who like to spend money to hire a designer."

—Touba Moore, Fort Collins, CO

"Finding clients, setting fees."

—Eva

"Number of balls in the air; employee issues."

—Anonymous 1

"Trying to juggle subcontractors and keep the accounts payable coming in for them in a timely manner."

—Anonymous 2

"Maintaining perspective and acquiring wealthy clients."

—Jeane Dole, Denver, CO

"Foreseeing complications in the process that were not covered in the original scope of the work agreement."

—Rey Viquez, III, Los Angeles, CA

"Keeping sales and marketing activities moving forward while focusing on completion of current projects."

—Rita Coltrane

Useful Skills from Previous Careers

"I was previously a consultant in the technology field and in environmental graphic design. I learned how to run a project and be diligent about follow up and follow through."

—Amy Haupl, Los Angeles, CA

"I worked for a Fortune 500 company and learned how to manage projects. I also did international marketing for the company."

—Anonymous 2

"I used to build furniture and now design it."

—Leslie Harris, Los Angeles, CA

"Set design is where I started my career and believe that really helps me set the energy and tone of a client's home."

—Studio 10, Denver CO

"I have a BS and MA in horticulture. I built a home and designed it, and then I went to design school."

—Touba Moore, Fort Collins, CO

"I sold real estate, which taught me how to negotiate."

—Anonymous 3, Englewood, CO

"I was a facilities architect and space planner."

—Anonymous 4

First Clients

"My first clients were my parents."

—Jean Zimmas, Santa Monica, CA

"I got my first client through staging a home show."

—Jean Dole, Denver, CO

"My first client called me. I went to my second client, a hospital, with a résumé. They hired me for a small project, liked that, and hired me for another small project and another larger project. Then, they fired the large design firm on a huge renovation and hired me for the five-year job. Yahoo!"

—Cynthia Greathouse

WHEN ARE YOUR CLIENTS MOST RELUCTANT TO PAY FOR SOMETHING?

"Clients are most reluctant to pay when the price point is high and they think they can find it cheaper themselves."

—Anonymous 2

"If they don't understand something. And my über-wealthy clients hate taxes on anything."

—Anonymous 4

"When it is an additional service fee."

—Anonymous 5

"At the end of a job."

—Anonymous 6

ON MARKETING

"I want to know how to market myself during this difficult economy."

—Jean Zimmas, Santa Monica, CA

"It is essential."

—Rey Viquez, III, Los Angeles, CA

What is your Marketing Strategy?

"I've been sending out MacBooks of my portfolio to possible clients."

—Leslie Harris, Los Angeles, CA

"Originally, I focused on marketing faux finishes. It was very custom, and clients needing faux finishes also needed other services. It was a great differentiator and door-opener."

—Rita Coltrane

About Specializing

"For fifteen years, my specialty has been color. I am a color expert. Two years ago, I began researching products for luxurious, green home furnishings, and thinking of that area for my specialty. Now, after your talk, I feel more inclined to head for universal design. Wheelchair accessibility and safety in the shower and bath are something I always mention to new clients, and several have remodeled accordingly. Personal experience with my brother, who lived in a wheelchair for thirty years, informs my understanding."

—Linda Adams, Montecito, CA

Who is Your Ideal Client?

"My ideal clients depend on design for the success of their business."

—Rey Viquez, III, Los Angeles, CA

"I've had a couple. They value your services, do not argue over fees, and refer lots of new clients."

—Anonymous 1

"An international client."

—Anonymous 5

"I had a client last year who had good taste, knew what she wanted, trusted my opinion, and could visualize (and had money)."

—Eva

"My ideal client says, 'Just do a good job, regardless of budget.'"

—Anonymous 6

"The project: space planning through full selection of materials and finishes through implementation. Perfect if client wants me to do everything—and they're not there."

—Jeane Dole, Denver, CO

Chapter 15: WHERE THE RUBBER MEETS THE ROAD

--- ❖ ---

As this book nears completion, the world economy is sliding into a recession which will most likely still be with us well after the release of this book. Moreover, the changes that are necessitated as a result of the financial crisis may well be permanent. To suggest that the playing field has changed is an understatement. Stephen Covey describes our current business environment as one of "white-water management." The turmoil of the surrounding waters is so loud you can't hear the other people in your raft who are trying to coordinate efforts to stay afloat, and the surface is always changing, so constant adjustments need to be made to course and paddling.

DEMOGRAPHICS AND DESIGN

While it would be easy to despair and perhaps change industries altogether, I don't think that's necessary. If you follow the signs, there are some obvious directions to take that I think will lead to future profits.

The industry as we know it today will be a vastly different landscape in 2009 and beyond. There are a number of demographic factors that are worth noting and through which designers will flourish when the economies rebound.

A resource that I have found invaluable is the "Environmental Scanning Report" issued by the American Society of Interior Designers on an annual basis. While the report is worth the full read (available to members at *www.asid.org*), I have extracted what I think are the most salient points (and their application to your career) from the 2008 report. The report was produced earlier in the year, and much has changed with respect to the world economy, with the failure of many banking institutions and the lowering of consumer confidence in general. Alas, these financial cycles happen. My focus is on what is needed when we cycle up again, as we will.

A MILLION MILLIONAIRES

By 2025, according to Outlook 2008 published by the World Future Society, the world will have a billion millionaires! That means that the rich are in fact getting richer and multiplying. While North America has the highest concentration of wealth today, it is recognized that populations of the wealthy are growing faster in developed and emerging markets in other parts of the world. A good acronym to become familiar with is BRIC, which stands for Brazil, Russia, India, and China. They are busy growing their economies and producing millionaires and billionaires, and will eventually surpass the U.S. in these numbers. It is imperative that businesses focus on the global marketplace for future clients, whether it is for design projects in the U.S. or elsewhere in the world.

LIVING LONGER

People are also living longer, especially those with money. By 2030, the number of people in the U.S. over 65 years of age will more than double. (There are similar statistics for other developed countries.)

The key forces that are radically altering medicine, such as nano-tech, neurotech, and genomics, are leading to longer and healthier lives. More importantly, this market segment is not content with sliding into retirement and watching TV. They want to continue enjoying their lives. They are getting out into the world, they are involved in their communities, and some of them have the money to fuel their passions.

Chances are many of these active seniors will be Asian and Hispanic. In fact, 12 percent of the U.S. population in 2004 was foreign-born. It is important to be aware of cultural differences and to recognize that what's normal in the U.S. may not be so to a consumer from another country. Many Asian cultures have extended families living with them, which requires expanded living spaces, special cooking facilities, and more. While this does not call for a wholesale alteration of business practice, a little sensitivity might go a long way.

THREE LIKELY GROWTH MARKETS

With these factors in mind, prudence dictates focusing on the high-end market, aging-in-place and universal design—and learning another language, as well, or at least hiring someone who speaks Spanish or an Asian language. These demographic changes are going to happen regardless of the economy today; they are permanent shifts. Look at your business today and decide what you need to do to meet the needs of your evolving clientele, from continuing education courses in design schools, study tours to other countries (the best way to learn about another country is to visit it), and cultural diversity courses.

World influence is shifting from the West to the East, with India and China poised to surpass the U.S. in economic dominance. The sheer numbers of their populations combined with their growing manufacturing and technology sectors make these nations likely to take the lead from the U.S. and other developed countries. India, largely because of its democratic government and transparent financial reporting, may well attract more financing and surpass China in economic dominance.

Meanwhile, the U.S. population is making a shift from the East to the West, with states like Nevada and Arizona being the fastest in growth and California still remaining the largest in population. An aging population tends to have a preference for warmer climates, so this shift is demographically determined. There's no reason why people need to live their entire lives in one area, particularly if their children have moved elsewhere and they want to be closer to them.

So, where do you think your next clients are coming from? What language will they be speaking? Perhaps opening an office in Scottsdale or Las Vegas is not be the worst decision you could make (think long-term). An interesting reality of the design business is that interior designers often follow their clients, doing multiple properties and projects, and developing resources in areas favored by their clients. Pay attention to the migratory routes people in your region follow, like New York to Florida, Texas to New Mexico, and California to Hawaii—and lots of ski resorts. As you work on your San Francisco client's house in Big Bear, you can keep your eyes out for other clients in the area. It makes sense to seek additional commissions in the region where you are working.

TARGETING GROWTH FIELDS

Ours is an economy of innovation and premiumization. Anything that involves Nano-bio-IT-neuro will be hot and garner a large portion of investment dollars. Research, development, marketing, and sales of the products and services developed in those four categories will be driving global economies. Moreover, they will radically alter the way we live. Targeting clients in technology, biotechnology, and medicine would be a wise choice. Designers have specialized in medical offices for many years and have transformed the look and feel of hospital environments, helping lower the level of anxiety patients feel when entering the spaces. Interior designers are poised to be the change agents of our time, helping guide their clients through the sea of technology, construction advances, and sustainability that make mere "decorating" the least of our concerns.

The wealthy have an inexhaustible need for anything that is exclusive, like limited-edition beer, "bespoke" artisanal chocolates, and customized vacation experiences that offer one-of-a-kind encounters. Companies are finding ways to refine their messaging and delivery to make the experience or product unique to each customer. The message will speak to one person and one person alone, much like having a suit tailored for the customer. While the style might be available to many, the particular material, buttons, cut, and stitching will be highly individualized. This trend is good for interior designers, who know how to tailor a room or a house to an individual.

CROSS-MARKETING

This leads to the topic of cross-marketing. We continue to see the collaboration between diverse brands, from luxury goods, lodging, transportation, financial services, technology—you name it. Nationally, there is a charity called DIFFA (Design Industry Fighting for AIDS) that combines design professionals with every major brand, including Tiffany, Continental Airlines, and Bank of America, creating living spaces that often incorporate the look and feel of the corporate partner. Reach out and find marketing partners who want to capture their share of the dollars that your clients are spending. This is non-competitive—something that stretches marketing dollars by sharing expenses across multiple budgets. Charities are superb at doing this; having just about everything contributed by a different sponsor. Using this model, prepare your next marketing campaign with some other partners: bring in the architect, contractor, and real estate agent as well.

SHARING VIRTUALLY AND ACTUALLY

When should you take these steps? That's easy: yesterday. With the Internet and social networking, everything is happening in real time. We now know what our friends are doing because they tell the world what they are up to at this very moment. Profiles are available to young and old alike, and e-mail is ubiquitous. Social networking is changing much more than the concept of a "friend." A high-end design client told me that he has gotten three projects through his MySpace (*www.myspace.com*) page. There seems to be a candor that happens when people start communicating electronically. They are sharing and seeking insights on life, people, and most importantly, products and services. The key is to not make your approach too commercial or sales-pitchy, but to just share something about who you are and a bit about your philosophy on things.

People are at once seeking exotic experiences and participating in events that give them opportunities to share time with friends and family. They are paying attention to the Internet and to design shows and makeovers on TV. They are also influenced by brand ambassadors and want to experience a product in an environment that enhances the usability and desirability of the product (think premium liquor at an event). There continues to be a drive towards authentic items, services, and a shared sense of values. Consumers want to know the lineage and environmental impact of the brands they are buying, in addition to the people (celebrities or their other rich friends) who are currently using the product. They also want a choice in the products and services that cater to their personal taste and style. Now more than ever, you need to have a business that "speaks" to your target market.

The next time you plan a trip to a foreign location, consider making part of it business and invite clients for the educational and shopping component so they can experience first-hand design inspiration and the process of pulling everything together to make the "magic" that is design. Or, taking a cue from the custom element of their furnishings, take a similar approach to other recommendations you make for their lifestyles, events they attend, homes they buy, and vacations they take. Everything is tailored, and concierge (lifestyle management) services are springing up for this reason. When guests return to a favorite hotel, the hotel remembers their preferences, including the types of pillows they enjoy and the water they like to drink.

THE TARGETED MESSAGE

Regardless of your specialty in design—contract, hospitality, residential, government, or institutional—your potential client stream has been fundamentally and radically altered, and so must be your approach to it. Consider how your marketing message needs to change so that it speaks directly to your target audience. Instead of thinking in terms of broad messages applied through mass media, think specific messages to key decision makers, like CEOs of one industry (biotechnology) or homeowners in a residential golf community with homes valued at $5 million and up, or advertising agency managers. When you can speak to their needs and identify problems unique to them and let them know you understand how to fix them, then you have their attention—and their business. You need to cater to the person who is reading your message. As you target the individual, not only can you tailor your message, but you can afford to spend some money on intelligent marketing. You might not be able to send a package to 5,000 names, but you can probably do so to the right fifty.

There is plenty of money in the economy; it is just being spent more judiciously. Make sure your firm is at the forefront of the movement to protect investments, increase real estate values through strategic design planning, and increase profits through enhanced employee morale. In making homes more livable and satisfying, what you are doing is not just good design. You are improving the quality of environments, managing lifestyles, and helping businesses thrive.

ATTITUDE AND GRATITUDE

Throughout the course of my career, I have had the pleasure of working with many terrific people. I was originally going to say "talented," but that isn't always the case. As a consultant, my ability to elevate people from any level—average or brilliant—is what I have to offer. In a sense, I'm not as interested in talent as I am in attitude. Fortunately, there has been a lot of good attitude—and gratitude—along the way.

In the past ten years, I have worked with many design professionals in the industry—people who have been managing their own businesses for twenty, thirty, and more than forty years and who were open to changing the way they approached their businesses so that they could get what they wanted and earn what they deserved. Joy Wood, for instance, attended a small group program that I gave at the Laguna Design Center, sponsored by ASID. Since then, she writes, "I have implemented several of Lloyd's policies and techniques, to which I attribute a nearly 30 percent increase in my 2006 business. The mechanics and philosophy he purveys are a proven value in my business, Mirage Interiors, now existing eighteen years. I only wish that I had had his positive input forty-two years ago, when I started as a novice interior designer. Since hearing his presentation at an ASID luncheon last summer and hearing him speak twice since, I have adjusted my billing format and 'dare' to quote charges deserved and earned."

CHANGING OLD HABITS

It is my clients' willingness to change existing habits and learn new, more rewarding habits that makes my work possible. So, it is with gratitude that I thank Joy and the many others who have been part of my journey so far.

Now, in all fairness, there are plenty of designers out there who have tried very hard to make their businesses work. They have applied themselves diligently, and with a positive attitude, without attaining success. It happens, and that is the nature of the beast. Much of what we do in business is trial and error; we test different approaches to our marketing, negotiations, and probably design as well. While I know that certain designers can be known for a look, they will still add new twists to a theme in order to re-articulate a design scheme.

ALL OF THE GLORY AND ALL OF THE BLAME

The design of a business is similar, requiring constant modifications and refinement until everything is operating in a manner that is bearable. I use this last word with trepidation because it almost sounds negative. However, in my experience and that of other entrepreneurs, even when business is good and there is money in the bank, there is always something that needs to be addressed or a decision to be made that is not altogether pleasant. This is part of being an entrepreneur: highs and lows, feast or famine, all of the glory and all of the blame.

Occasionally when I am recruiting for a firm, I try to imagine myself working full-time at another company, and I giggle to myself, reflecting that I am now possibly unemployable, since I've been self-employed for ten years or so. It's an amazing experience running my own company, being responsible for payroll, rents, developing strategy, and bringing in business, as well as working for my clients. At the end of the day, the "buck stops here," and I'm solely responsible for the success or failure of my firm. It's a daunting task to be responsible for the livelihoods of other people, including their career growth and development. To do it right takes persistence, patience, vision, and integrity. I do look back at certain clients that I have advised and wish I had advised them differently. I also wish I had not worked at all with certain clients: it was not a good match for either of us. I've learned to trust my instincts and follow my gut—that little voice inside is always right.

THIS CRAZY BUSINESS

I'll finish with a story I just heard from Sarah Gallop, a friend and former account manager, which reinforces the crazy nature of our industry and why I love it so much. There is certain rug vendor who placed an order in Nepal for custom Aubusson rugs to be used throughout a palace in the Middle East. Alas, as does happen from time to time, the order was delayed. Enraged by this situation, the client contacted the vendor in New York and said that he was connected with the Russian mafia. If his rugs were not delivered on time, he would have the vendor and his entire family killed. The vendor opted to move to Nepal, where the rugs were being woven, to make sure that they were ready on time. The family came along for the experience—and for their safety.

And you think *your* clients are demanding?

Happy designing!

INDEX

❖

Books from Allworth Press

Allworth Press is an imprint of Allworth Communications, Inc. Selected titles are listed below.

Starting Your Career as an Interior Designer
by Robert K. Hale and Thomas L. Williams (paperback, 6 × 9, 256 pages, $24.95)

The Challenge of Interior Design: Professional Values and Opportunities
by Mary V. Knackstedt (paperback, 6 × 9, 272 pages, $24.95)

How to Start and Operate Your Own Design Firm: A Guide for Interior Designers and Architects, Second Edition
by Albert W. Rubeling, Jr., FAIA (paperback, 6 × 9, 256 pages, $24.95)

Business and Legal Forms for Interior Designers
by Tad Crawford and Eva Doman Bruck (paperback, 8 ½ × 11, 240 pages, $29.95)

The Interior Designer's Guide to Pricing, Estimating, and Budgeting
by Theo Stephan Williams (paperback, 6 × 9, 208 pages, $19.95)

How to Think Like a Great Graphic Designer
by Debbie Millman (paperback, 6 × 9, 248 pages, $24.95)

The Graphic Designer's Guide to Better Business Writing
by Barbara Janoff and Ruth Cash-Smith (paperback, 6 × 9, 256 pages, $19.95)

Creating the Perfect Design Brief: How to Manage Design for Strategic Advantage
by Peter L. Phillips (paperback, 6 × 9, 224 pages, $19.95)

The Graphic Design Business Book
by Tad Crawford (paperback, 6 × 9, 256 pages, $24.95)

Graphic Designer's Guide to Clients: How to Make Clients Happy and Do Great Work
by Ellen Shapiro (paperback, 6 × 9, 256 pages, $19.95)

AIGA Professional Practices in Graphic Design, Second Edition
edited by Tad Crawford (paperback, 6 × 9, 336 pages, $29.95)

Designing Logos: The Process of Creating Logos That Endure
by Jack Gernsheimer (paperback, 8 ½ × 10, 208 pages, $35.00)

Designing Effective Communications: Creating Contexts for Clarity and Meaning
edited by Jorge Frascara (paperback, 6 × 9, 304 pages, 100 b&w illustrations, $24.95)

To request a free catalog or order books by credit card, call 1-800-491-2808. To see our complete catalog on the World Wide Web, or to order online for a 20 percent discount, you can find us at **www.allworth.com.**